STITCH
ALPHABETS
& NUMBERS

××× ——

120 contemporary Designs for Cross Stitch and Needlepoint

Felicity Hall

David and Charles

www.stitchcraftcreate.co.uk

CONTENTS

INTRODUCTION

I am extremely passionate about needlepoint and the art of stitching and always try to create designs that will be fun to do and keep your interest, but also fit with stylish interiors – I don't want all of your hard work to end up at the bottom of a cupboard never to be seen by anyone! It's important that you are proud of what you have stitched and can exclaim at the top of your voice, 'I made it myself!'. It is so rewarding taking time to make something physical, from a simple stitch, piece of fabric, needle and some lengths of thread. I truly believe that there is nothing more satisfying than creating something yourself and enjoying the end result as much as the process of making it.

This book has been created to allow you to use the charted cross stitch designs in a variety of different ways, and to inspire you to create your own individual pieces and experiment with different fabrics and threads, showing that there is a range of effective ways you can stitch the charts to create larger or smaller items.

You can choose your own alternative colourways for any of the charts, giving you the freedom to change the look of each design. Each letter and number collection has been designed so that you can stitch them separately or combine them to make dates and words. The larger designs are approximately 80 x 80 stitches and the smaller ones are generally about 55 x 55 stitches. There is also a selection of corner designs and ampersands, which can be mixed and matched with each collection.

The materials and equipment you will need are described in the next section, followed by a chapter explaining the stitches and techniques used. The projects all use a variety of different fabrics and different types of thread and wool - see the end of the book for details. Thread conversion tables are given at the end of the chart sections of the book, allowing you to change to different thread brands if you wish.

MATERIALS & EQUIPMENT

FABRICS

The type of fabric you choose to work with can really change the look of your finished piece. There is an excellent selection of canvas and coloured Aida and evenweave available. My preference is always the Zweigart brand as it's very good quality. Generally, if you use canvas then you need to stitch the background as well; if you use an Aida or evenweave there is no need to – so less work!

Evenweave – This is a term used to describe a fabric or canvas where the number of threads per square inch/centimetre is the same for both the warp and weft. When a fabric is titled 'evenweave' it is usually woven with a single thread, so for cross stitch you usually stitch over two of the fabric threads.

Aida – This is an evenweave fabric woven with the threads grouped into bundles to form a square pattern, which in turn creates easily visible holes. This type of fabric is normally stitched over one block. 'Binca' is an Aida fabric that has large holes and so is great for beginners.

Canvas – This is a stiff, open-weave fabric. Single thread canvas is available in two varieties called mono canvas and interlock canvas. Mono canvas is plain woven with a single warp and weft thread passing over and under each other. Interlock canvas is woven with the warp and the weft threads twisted around each other where they intersect. This construction 'locks' the canvas in place and makes it very stable and stiff. The most common mesh sizes for single thread canvas are 10hpi, 12hpi, 14hpi and 18hpi.

Plastic canvas – This lightweight canvas is made of moulded plastic with holes in a grid formation and is usually sold in pre-cut sheets. Its rigidity makes it perfect for three-dimensional projects.

CROSS STITCH TERMS

Hpi – This stands for holes per inch. It is also called the 'gauge' of a fabric or its 'count'. If you are unsure what hpi your fabric is, take a ruler and count how many holes there are in a linear inch. i.e., a 14 hpi fabric has 14 holes per inch. Remember, the higher the hpi the smaller the finished design; the lower the hpi the larger the design.

14 holes = 14 hpi (holes per inch)

Ply – The number of strands twisted to form the thread, for example, a 4-ply thread has four strands twisted together.

CALCULATING FABRIC AMOUNTS

It is useful to be able to work out the size of fabric you will require, and in turn the size the design will be when stitched on different fabrics. To convert inches to centimetres, multiply the inch measurement by 2.54.

- To calculate the height of the design (in inches), divide the design's height in stitches by the holes per inch (hpi) of the fabric.

- To calculate the width of the design (in inches), divide the design's width in stitches by the holes per inch (hpi) of the fabric.

80 stitches high

÷ 14 hpi = 5.7 inches high

÷ 14 hpi = 5.7 inches wide

80 stitches wide

THREADS

There is a huge variety of threads for needlework and using different types of thread can give totally different effects. For example, stranded cotton creates a lovely delicate appearance, whereas 4-ply tapestry wool creates a chunky, soft look. You can also achieve different effects by mixing different threads and fabrics. For example, if you use a finer thread on a higher hpi fabric then the crosses of the cross stitch will appear clearer; if you use a thicker thread then the crosses will appear more like a padded square. Different projects may suit different effects and ultimately it is your own preference. Some of my favourite threads are described here. They are all widely available in a variety of colours.

Stranded cotton   This is also called floss and is a slightly twisted, slightly glossy six-stranded (6-ply) cotton thread. The six-stranded skeins are divisible, so you can use different numbers of strands depending on the look you want to achieve and the type/hpi of fabric you are using. Two strands are normally used on 14 hpi Aida fabric.

Tapestry wool – This is available in two sizes, 4-ply and 2-ply, both non-divisible. The 4-ply size is a tightly twisted pure wool, perfect for cross stitching cushions using canvas. The 2-ply size is finer and is also known as crewel wool. It's great for smaller pieces.

Perle cotton – This is a 2-ply non-divisible twisted cotton thread with a high sheen. It is available in a range of thicknesses – 3, 5 and 8 are the most common. The lower the number, the thicker the thread.

TIP Measure your fabric accurately and allow at least a 5cm (2in) margin of fabric around your design.

TIP Colour conversion tables for different thread brands are given at the back of the book. You could also ask at your local needlework shop, or go to www.felicityhall.co.uk

CALCULATING THREAD AMOUNTS

If you want to calculate thread amounts for every colour in a design see the formula below. There are also tables on my website at: www.felicityhall.co.uk or www.stitchcraftcreate.co.uk. The formula below gives thread amounts in skeins for the main manufacturers. To convert centimetres to inches, divide centimetres by 2.54.

- Take a 20cm length of your chosen type of thread and stitch as many cross stitches in a block as you can from that length of thread on your chosen type of fabric (make sure this is exactly the same hpi as you want to use for the design).

- On the website, pick a colour from the table, divide the total amount of stitches by the number of stitches you have managed to stitch from your 20cm (8in) length.

- Multiply this number by 20 to find the total amount of that colour needed in centimetres. Add on 100cm (40in) to make sure you will have enough.

20cm

Total number of stitches of one shade ÷ ? (number of stitches worked from a 20cm length) x 20 = amount of thread needed in centimetres + 100 (extra to be safe)

WOOL/THREAD AMOUNTS

Wool/thread	Amount
Appleton Tapestry Wool	1 skein = 10m
	1 hank = 55m
DMC Tapestry Wool	1 skein = 8m
Anchor Tapestry Wool	1 skein = 10m
DMC Stranded Cotton	1 skein = 8m
Anchor Stranded Cotton	1 skein = 8m

EQUIPMENT

Very little equipment is required for cross stitch embroidery – the following tools will be most useful.

TAPESTRY NEEDLE

This needle is blunt-ended, which avoids splitting the threads of the fabric. Tapestry needles are available in sizes 14 to 26, and the larger the number of the needle, the smaller the size/diameter of the needle. Every stitcher has their preference for needles. I use size 20 for wool/canvas work and size 22–24 for stranded cotton/Aida. The main thing to remember is that you need the needle big enough to pass the thread easily through the eye, but small enough to not distort the fabric. The table gives needle sizes for various holes per inch.

13 14 16 18 20 22 24

Higher number = smaller needle

CHOOSING NEEDLE SIZES FOR FABRICS

Fabric hpi	Needle size
10	20
14	24
18	28

TIP When using wool on size 10 or 14 hpi canvas, use needle size 20.

NEEDLE THREADER

A threader is optional, but there are some very good solid metal yarn threaders available on the market, which can save a lot of time and frustration! The diagram shows how to use one.

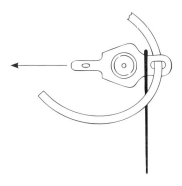

SCISSORS

Invest in a really good pair of sharp embroidery scissors and a pair of dress-making scissors for cutting your fabrics.

SHADE CARD

It is a good idea to either make or buy a plastic shade card thread organizer, which helps to keep things simple and makes it easy to read the charts and also distinguish each symbol/thread colour.

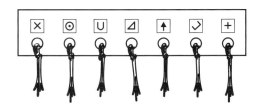

MASKING TAPE

This is useful as it can be folded over fabric edges to stop any fraying while you work. Remove it on completion of the project.

LIGHTING

Always work in good light. Daylight is the best, but if you like to work in the evenings invest in a daylight lamp.

EMBROIDERY HOOPS AND FRAMES

The purpose of a frame or hoop is to hold the fabric taut during stitching. These are completely optional, as the nature of cross stitch means that the fabric won't distort too much. Some stitchers prefer to use a frame or hoop as it makes it easier to keep your stitches neat. Hoops come in many sizes and may be hand-held or attached to a stand. They can also be used to display your work in, as seen in some of the projects featured. Frames are good for larger projects, especially the easy clip variety as it's easier to move your work on and off the frame.

Embroidery hoops are best for lighter fabrics

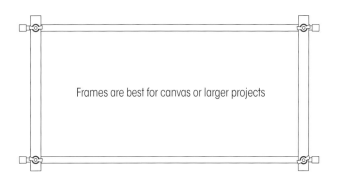

Frames are best for canvas or larger projects

STITCHES & TECHNIQUES

READING CROSS STITCH CHARTS

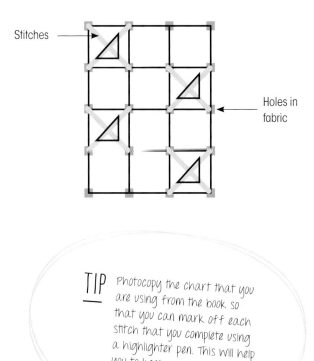

Stitches

Holes in fabric

- Each coloured square and symbol on the chart represents one fabric mesh covered by one cross stitch (see diagrams).

- Each symbol represents a different colour. The chart key is repeated on every two-page spread of the charted sections of the book. Alternative colourways (where provided) are at the end of the design sections.

- The major grid lines are slightly darker in 10 x 10 sections to make reading the chart and keeping your place easier.

- The centre of the chart is indicated by arrows. Always start stitching from the centre of a design and always count the grid squares carefully to help keep track of where you are.

- To find the centre of your fabric, fold it into quarters and mark the middle with backstitched lines – this is called tracking. If working on canvas with wool you could use a permanent marker, but not if your background is white as it will show through.

TIP Photocopy the chart that you are using from the book so that you can mark off each stitch that you complete using a highlighter pen. This will help you to keep count.

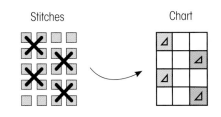

Stitches   Chart

CREATING LONGER WORDS, NAMES OR DATES

I would suggest that you photocopy each letter/number and then stick all the charts together to form your design, as this will make it a lot easier to read the chart and work from the centre. The spacing of the letters/numbers is completely up to you, however, I find most of them work best when they are positioned close together, say six or seven stitches apart. Play around with your photocopies until you are happy with the overall look – just make sure all of the letters are lined up. The only exception to this is the screen-printed numbers, as these look best when the black numbers are lined up, not the coloured area.

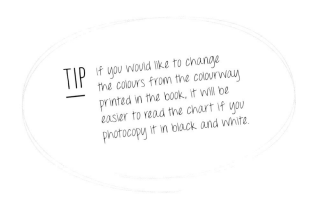
WASTE KNOT METHOD

Thread your needle and make a knot at the end. Take the needle through the right side of the fabric a couple of centimetres/inch away from where you would like to start stitching. If you are stitching right to left, take the needle through the fabric to the left of where you are about to start and then start stitching, working over the thread at the back. When the thread is secure, snip off the knot at the front.

USING THE CORNER BORDER DESIGNS

Some borders have been designed as corner pieces, to provide you with additional decorative elements. Again, you can photocopy them and cut out so that you can arrange your design easily. Make sure to mirror image the design on the photocopier for opposite corners.

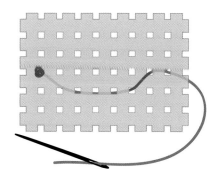

BEGINNING TO STITCH

There are a few ways to start stitching. I leave about a 2.5cm (1in) of loose thread at the back of the fabric, hold it with the forefinger of my left hand (I'm right-handed) and work the first few stitches over it to secure the thread.

KNOTLESS LOOP METHOD

Starting this way is very useful if you are using more than one strand of thread doubled up in the needle (but only if you are using an even number of strands). Begin stitching and bring the needle up through the fabric leaving a loop at the back of it. Put the needle back through the fabric, passing the needle through the loop – this will secure the thread so you can continue stitching.

WORKING A SINGLE CROSS STITCH

Bring your needle up at position 1 on the diagram, then down at 2, up at 3 and down at 4. Note how the top thread of the cross is formed from lower left to upper right – this is the traditional direction, but it really doesn't matter as long as all of your stitches are the same.

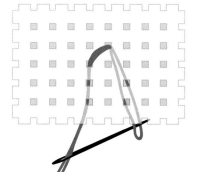

WORKING A LINE OF CROSS STITCHES

Work a line of cross stitches in two journeys, beginning at the right. Bring the needle up at position 1 on the diagram, then down at 2, up at 3, down at 4, up at 5, down at 6, and so on.

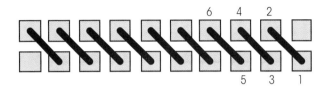

Now starting from the left side of the line, bring the needle up at 19, down at 20, up at 21, down at 22, and so on, crossing the existing stitches.

BLOCKING A FINISHED PIECE

Don't worry if your finished stitching has distorted the fabric slightly. Stitched pieces can be dampened, stretched and pulled back into shape – this is called blocking. To block your stitching all you need is a piece of plywood at least 5cm (2in) larger than your finished design fabric and some rustproof nails or carpet tacks.

1 Lay your completed work face down and dampen thoroughly by spraying it with water – a water mister for plants is perfect for this.

2 Place the stitching face down on the plywood board and slart to stretch the fabric back to its original shape.

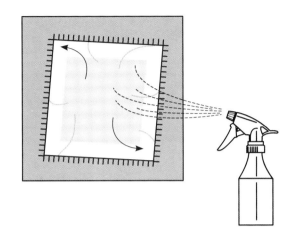

3 Start by hammering a nail into the centre of each side and then work out towards the corners. Let the fabric dry completely before removing it.

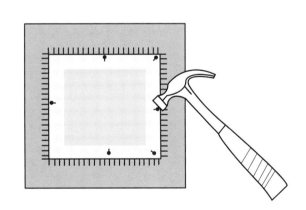

TIP If you are using fine fabric, such as Aida or evenweave, you may not need to use nails to secure the work. Simply dampen slightly and re-shape, and then press with an iron, making sure you protect your stitches with a piece of fabric.

MAKING UP

✗✗✗

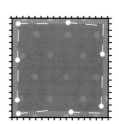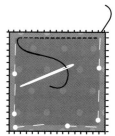

MAKING UP A CUSHION

I tend to stitch all the way around the outside of my cushions and don't bother adding fiddly zips. I find that if the cushion gets dirty you can easily sponge wash them to remove any marks using a gentle cleanser.

1 Begin by choosing a backing fabric for your design. Choose something quite durable with a tight weave – upholstery fabrics work best.

2 Trim your blocked cross stitched design to size so that you have about 2.5cm (1in) of extra fabric around the outside. Cut your backing fabric to match. If you would like to add a zip it is best to do it at this stage, along one of the edges.

4 Stitch around three of the sides. If your finished piece is stitched in wool on canvas, stitch around the outside on three sides one cross stitch in from the edge (this ensures that you don't see any of the white canvas once it's turned inside out).

5 Turn the cover right side out and stuff with a cushion pad. Hand stitch the opening closed.

ADDING PIPING

Piping can really add the finishing touch to a cushion. The easiest way to make your own is to use bias binding. This is a ready-made tape made from lengths of material cut on the bias, so that it stretches smoothly around corners. It is usually sold by the metre/yard and you can purchase it in an array of colours and patterns and in different thicknesses and fabrics. The piping is best added before you stitch on your backing fabric.

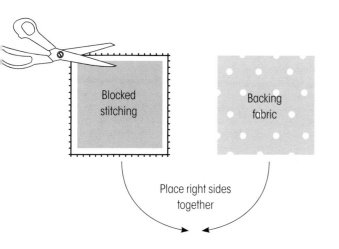

Blocked stitching

Backing fabric

Place right sides together

3 Place your cross stitch piece and backing fabric together so that the right sides are facing, and pin together around the edge.

TIP Try using two different sizes of piping on one cushion. This layered effect can look very striking and really set off a design beautifully.

1 To make piping, fold the bias binding over some upholstery cord or piping cord and hand sew tight against the cord, as shown in the diagram. Alternatively, use the zipper foot on your machine to sew along the edge.

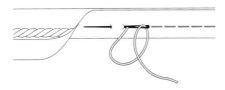

2 Tack (baste) the covered cord along the edge of your cross stitched piece. If it is a wool and canvas piece, sew it one stitch in from the edge. Join the cord at a corner, preferably on the bottom side of the cushion.

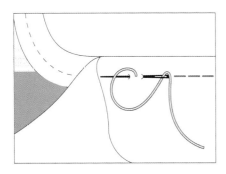

3 Pin and tack the backing fabric over the covered cord, so that the right side of the cross stitch and the right side of the backing fabric are facing. Stitch along the outside edge of the piping, as close as possible to the cord, for three sides, leaving one side open to stuff the cushion.

4 Turn right side out and stuff with a cushion pad. Hand stitch along the open edge, folding in the selvedge fabric.

TIP You can add any type of trim with a flange using the method just described. Stitch it onto the right side of the design first, making sure the flange is facing outwards.

FRAMING DESIGNS

Framing your designs is an easy way to display all of your hard work. It is up to you whether you cover your stitching with glass. I prefer to be able to see the stitches, but glass can help to protect your work. If you choose to use glass it is best to add a mount board as that way the glass will not touch the stitching. The easiest way to mount work for framing is to use foam board, which is board constructed of foam sandwiched between two layers of acid-free card.

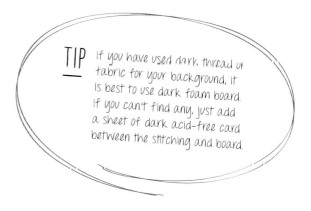

TIP If you have used dark thread or fabric for your background, it is best to use dark foam board. If you can't find any, just add a sheet of dark acid-free card between the stitching and board.

1 Cut a piece of foam board to fit inside your chosen frame, cutting it slightly smaller than your blocked stitching to allow room for the fabric and pins.

Blocked stitching

Foam board

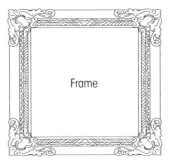

Frame

2 Position your design centrally over the foam board. Fold the corner over, as shown. Using stainless steel flat-headed pins, secure the stitching to the foam board by pushing a pin into the foam part of the board at the centre of each side. Repeat along each edge, gradually working out from the centre pin and gently pulling the fabric tight as you go. Keep checking that your work is still central.

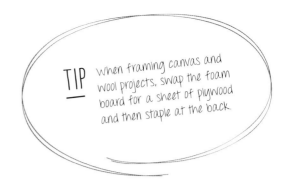

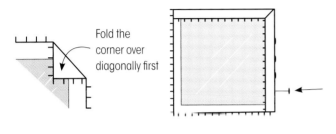

Fold the corner over diagonally first

3 Once all the edges have pins along them, mitre the corners neatly and secure using a few stitches. At this stage you could also lace across the back, as shown, to make the work more secure.

FRAMING IN A HOOP

Framing a piece in an embroidery hoop is really simple and can be very effective, especially for circular designs. Wooden embroidery hoops look best. You can also add colour and interest by wrapping the hoop with bias binding or strips of fabric.

1 Take your chosen embroidery hoop and trace the inner edge of the outer hoop onto a piece of felt using a pencil (if you are using a dark colour, use a white pencil). Cut out using scissors, following the inside of the line.

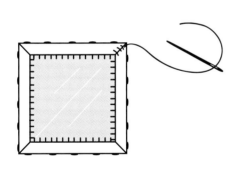

2 Place the finished cross stitch over the inner hoop and securely cover with the outer hoop, making sure the cross stitch is neatly stretched and centred, smoothing out any wrinkles. Tighten up the nut.

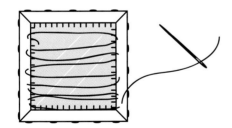

4 Place the work in the frame and cover with the backboard. Tape up the back using brown gum tape.

> **TIP** When framing canvas and wool projects, swap the foam board for a sheet of plywood and then staple at the back.

3 Trim the edges of your cross stitch fabric, within 2–3cm (¾–1¼in) of the outer hoop. If you are worried about the edges fraying then you can oversew or use a seam sealant. Press in the edges using an iron, so that they are folded in towards the centre of the ring.

4 Place the felt circle cut earlier against the back of the hoop. Using a whip stitch, hand sew the backing fabric to the hoop, catching the needle in the cross stitch fabric and the backing as you go.

MAKING AN ALPHABET BLOCK

The best designs to make an alphabet block are the woodcut letters, as they are already created within a square, but all of the designs in this book can be adapted and framed with the borders to create square designs. To make an alphabet block you need to work on plastic canvas as this will give the block the added rigidity you need for creating a three-dimensional object. You can stitch a letter or number on each side of the block or alternatively, use fabric on the other five sides. Stitched stripes in the same colours as the letter or number also work well.

TIP If you add a bell in the centre of the block, it can also be used as a baby's rattle.

1 Stitch your chosen designs onto six pieces of plastic canvas. Cut each one out so they measure the same size. Alternatively, if you only want one side to be stitched, cut out five squares of felt to match your stitched design and attach squares of plastic canvas to each square for rigidity, with a few stitches on each edge.

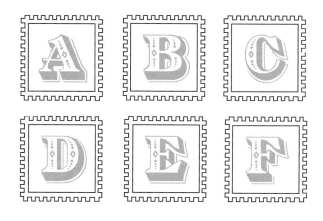

2 Lay your squares out as shown in the diagram.

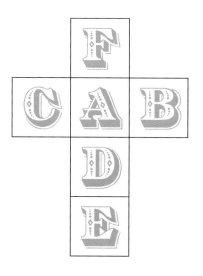

3 Stitch each square together using a whip stitch and matching thread, following the holes in the canvas along each edge. Leave one side open.

4 Fill the block with toy stuffing through the open side and then stitch up the side.

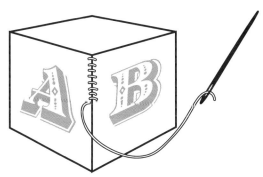

TIP Fill the cube with sand or gravel to create a heavy doorstop or a set of bookends.

MAKING A STRETCH CANVAS

This is one of the easiest ways to present your finished stitching. Ready-made artist's canvases are widely available in a variety of shapes and sizes. Alternatively, you can make your own frame and cover with a calico or artist's canvas.

1 Choose or make a canvas that will fit your finished piece. If the canvas is un-primed I suggest painting it with a white acrylic primer paint, which helps to tighten the canvas and gives the stitching a stable base to rest on.

2 Lay your blocked finished stitching over the canvas and position it so that it is centred. Carefully pin it in place.

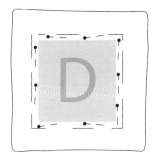

3 Turn the canvas over and staple or tack (baste) the stitched piece to the canvas frame In the middle of each side by folding over the excess fabric. Remove the pins and gradually work out from the middle staple, attaching the fabric and leaving the corners free. Keep checking that your design is square – if it's slightly pulled out of place, remove the staple and re-adjust.

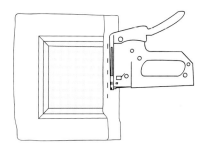

4 Attach the corners by folding the excess fabric from one side upwards, so it is tight against the frame and staple in place. Create a fold (like a hospital corner) and turn the other side up, to create a neat, square corner.

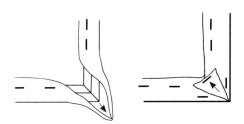

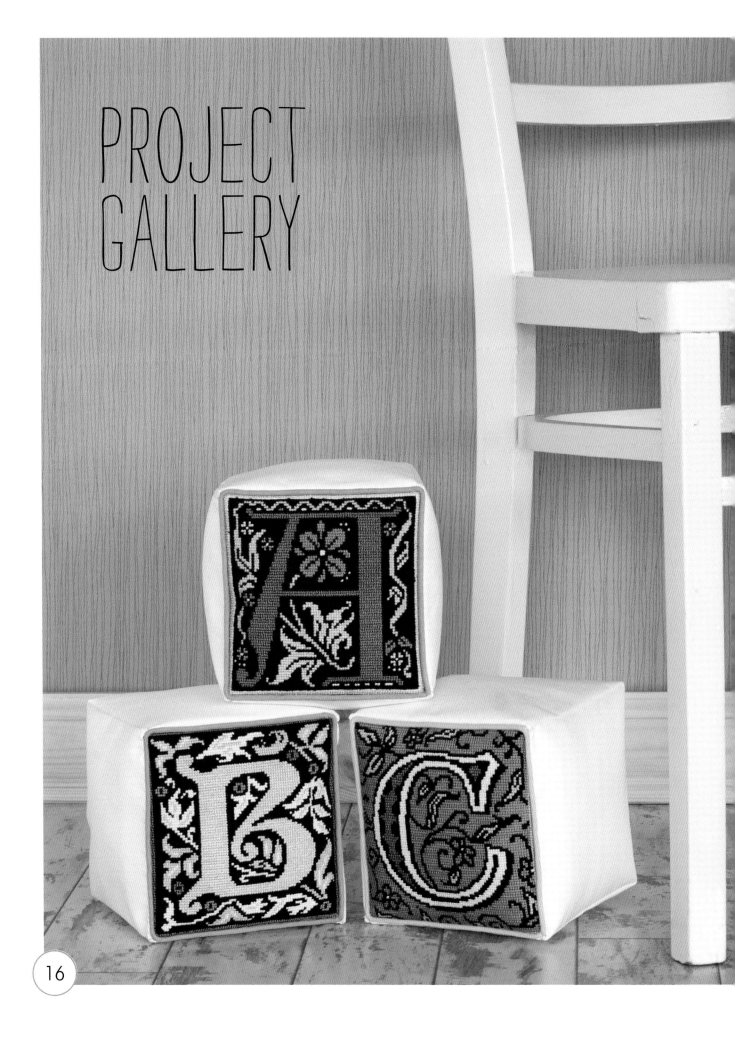

PROJECT
GALLERY

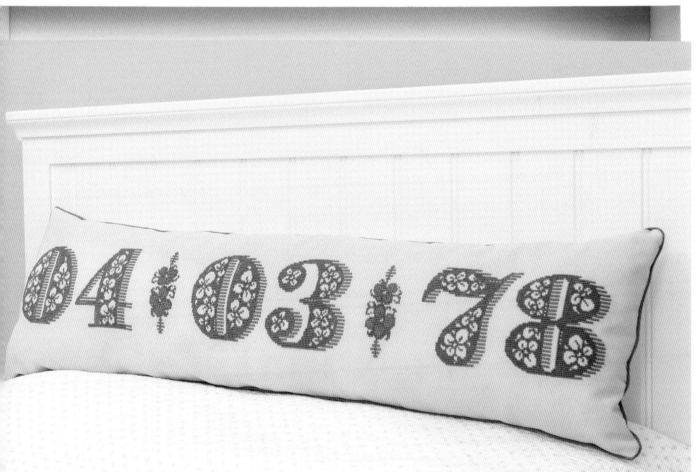

CIRCUS LETTERS

Inspired by the eccentric cheeky fonts found at circuses these designs can be used alone to create a statement initial cushion, or together to form names or words. The bold outlines and block colours are a joy to stitch, evolving quickly. For a larger design, team with the circus corner border, or keep it simple and stitch on a white background fabric. For alternate threads see Thread Conversion Tables.

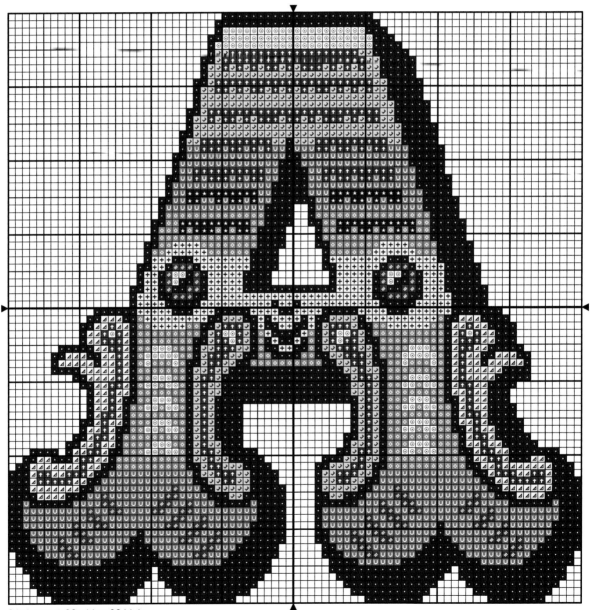

Stitch count: 80 wide x 80 high

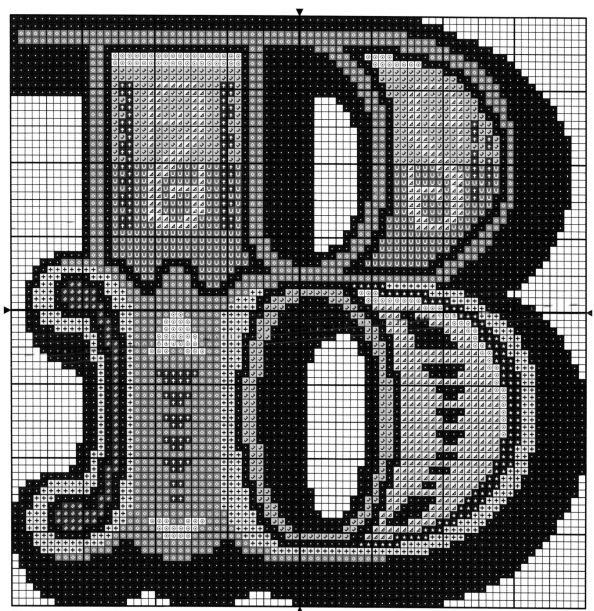

Stitch count: 80 wide x 80 high

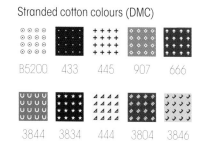

IDEA... For a simpler look work on Aida and just stitch the brown outlines and leave the background free of stitching.

Stranded cotton colours (DMC)

B5200	433	445	907	666
3844	3834	444	3804	3846

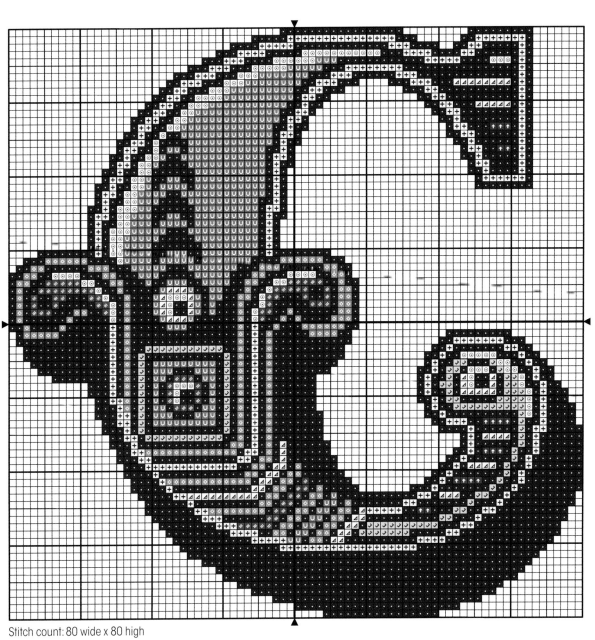

Stitch count: 80 wide x 80 high

Stranded cotton colours (DMC)

B5200   433   445   907   666   3844   3834   444   3804   3846

Stitch count: 80 wide x 80 high

Stitch count: 69 wide x 80 high

Stranded cotton colours (DMC)

B5200   433   445   907   666   3844   3834   444   3804   3846

Stitch count: 78 wide x 80 high

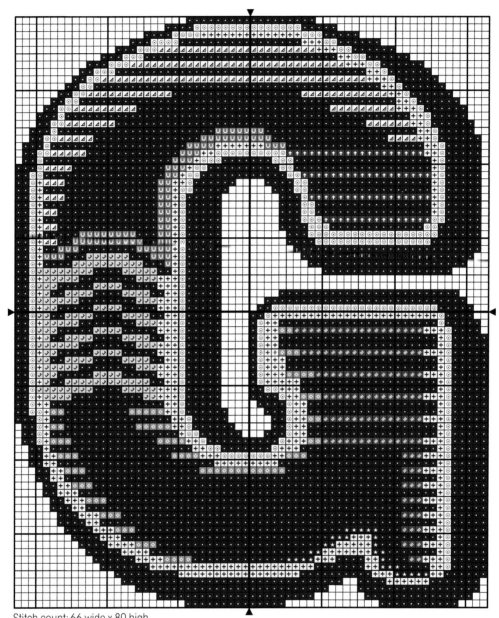

Stitch count: 66 wide x 80 high

Stranded cotton colours (DMC)

B5200　433　445　907　666　3844　3834　444　3804　3846

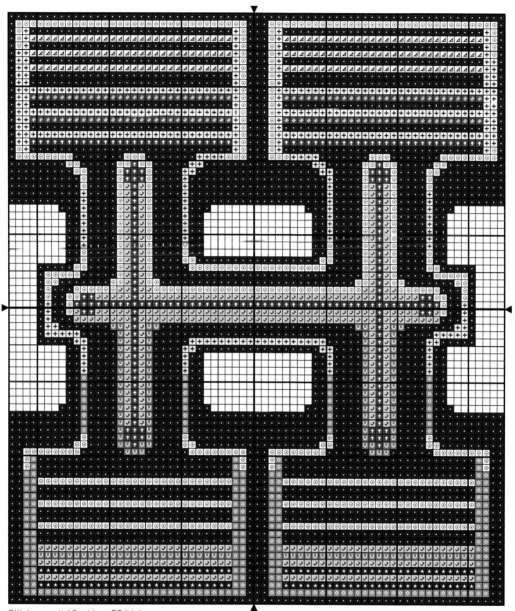

Stitch count: 69 wide x 80 high

IDEA... Add colourful piping or pompom trim to the edge of the design to up the fun factor.

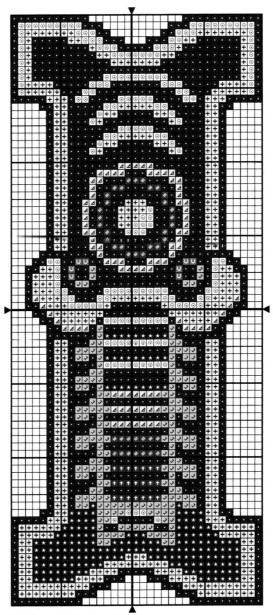

Stitch count: 35 wide x 80 high

Stranded cotton colours (DMC)

B5200	433	445	907	666	3844	3834	444	3804	3846

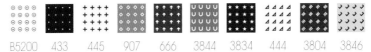

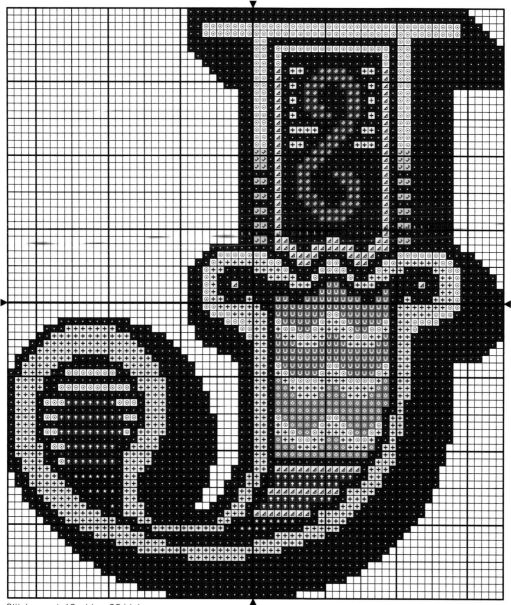

Stitch count: 69 wide x 80 high

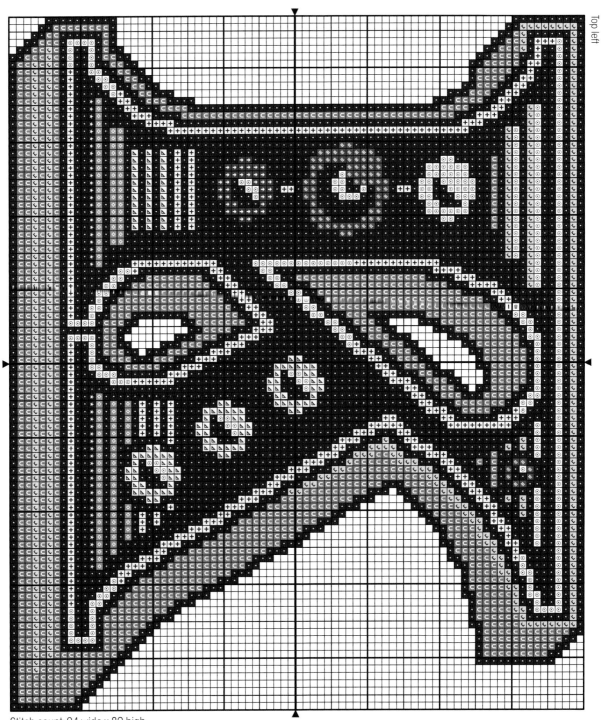

Stitch count: 94 wide x 80 high

Stranded cotton colours (DMC)

B5200   433   445   907   666   3844   3834   444   3804   3846

Stitch count: 85 wide x 80 high

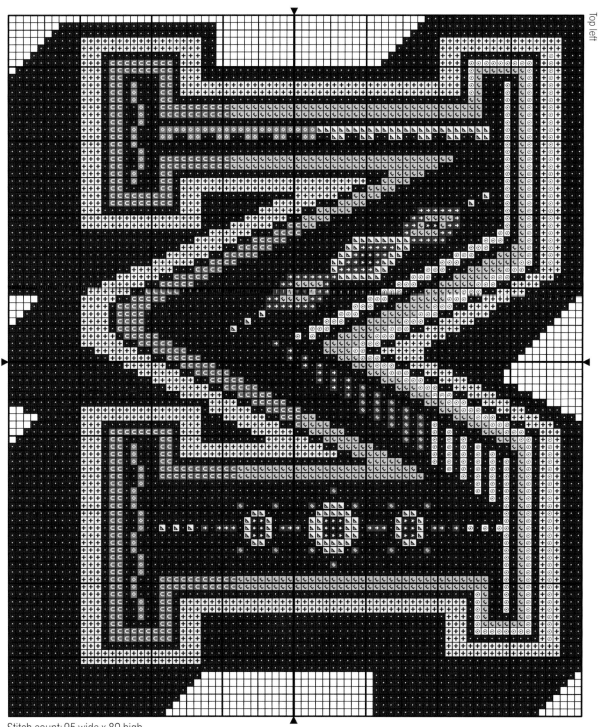

Stitch count: 95 wide x 80 high

Stranded cotton colours (DMC)

B5200	433	445	907	666	3844	3834	444	3804	3846

Stitch count: 69 wide x 80 high

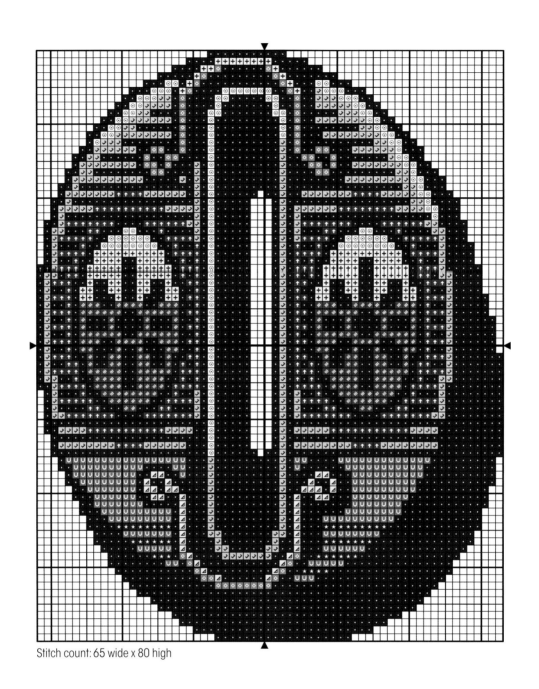

Stitch count: 65 wide x 80 high

Stranded cotton colours (DMC)

B5200   433   445   907   666   3844   3834   444   3804   3846

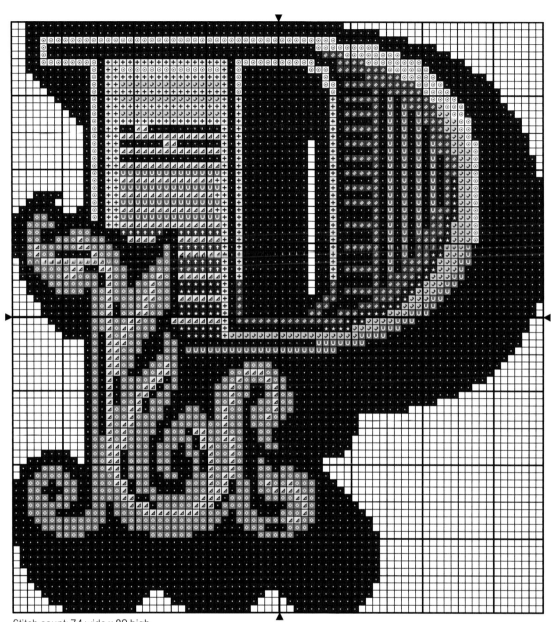

Stitch count: 74 wide x 80 high

IDEA... At home on a grown-up sitting room sofa or on a child's bed, these playful letters will add an element of cheekiness to any interior.

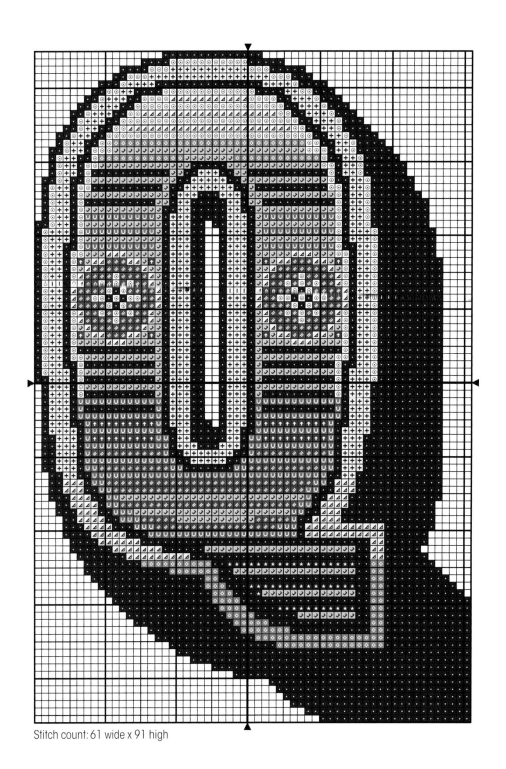

Stitch count: 61 wide x 91 high

Stranded cotton colours (DMC)

B5200   433   445   907   666   3844   3834   444   3804   3846

Top left

Stitch count: 91 wide x 80 high

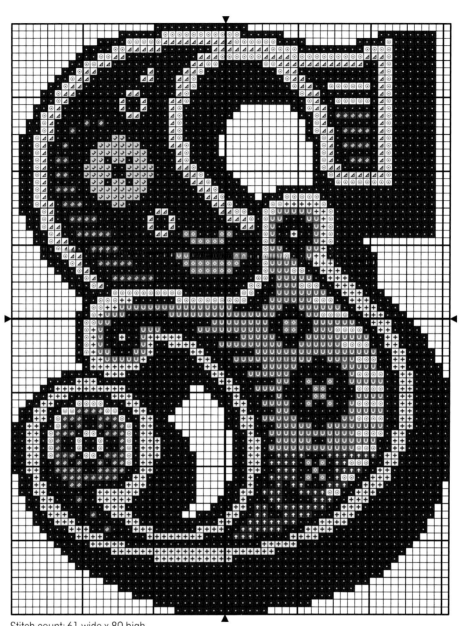

Stitch count: 61 wide x 80 high

Stranded cotton colours (DMC)

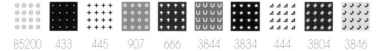

B5200   433   445   907   666   3844   3834   444   3804   3846

Stitch count: 60 wide x 80 high

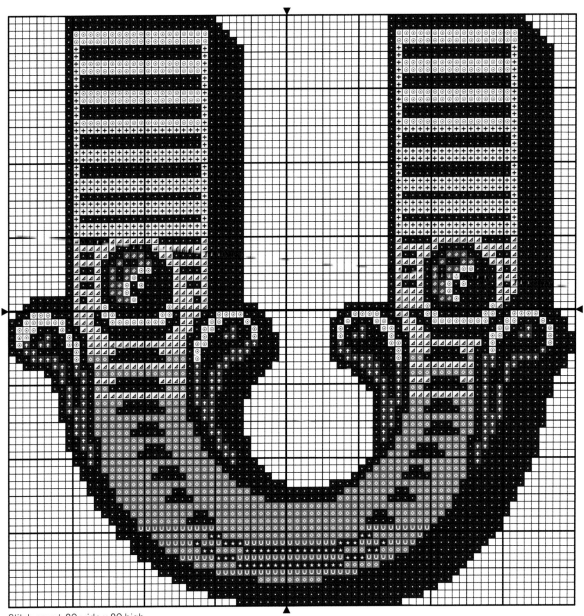

Stitch count: 80 wide x 80 high

Stranded cotton colours (DMC)

B5200 433 445 907 666 3844 3834 444 3804 3846

Stitch count: 80 wide x 80 high

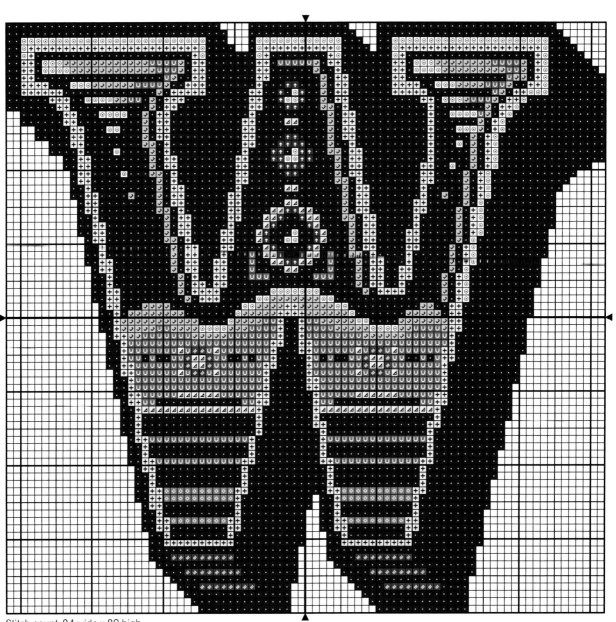

Stitch count: 84 wide x 80 high

Stranded cotton colours (DMC)

B5200	433	445	907	666	3844	3834	444	3804	3846

Stitch count: 51 wide x 80 high

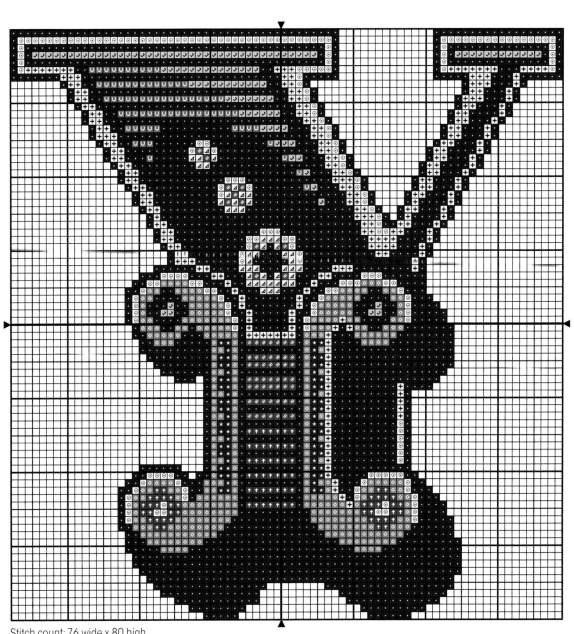

Stitch count: 76 wide x 80 high

Stranded cotton colours (DMC)

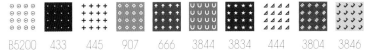

| B5200 | 433 | 445 | 907 | 666 | 3844 | 3834 | 444 | 3804 | 3846 |

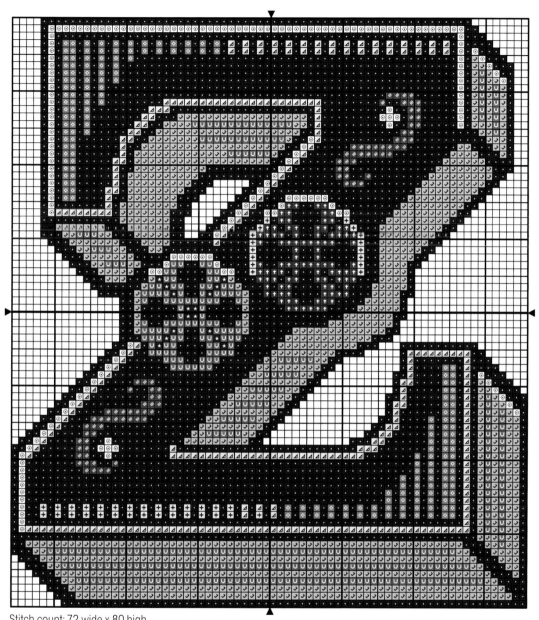

Stitch count: 72 wide x 80 high

IDEA... Create a playful version by stitching the letters in fun colours, or use a monochrome palette for an understated stylish accent.

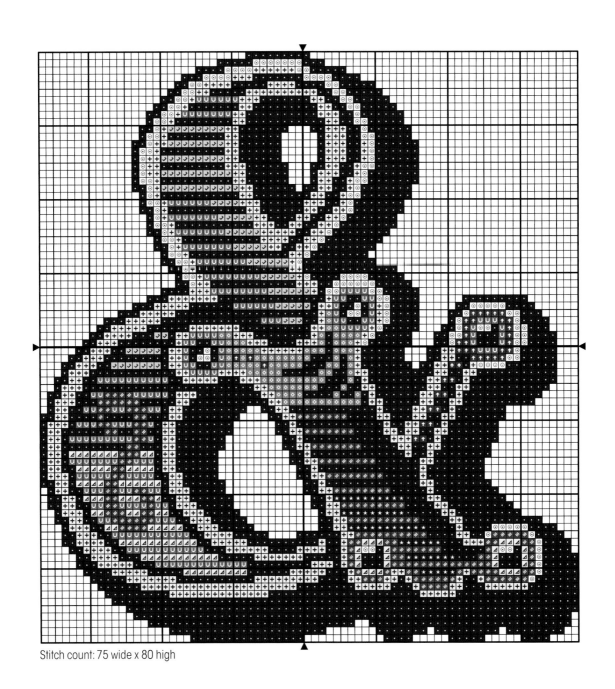

Stitch count: 75 wide x 80 high

Stranded cotton colours (DMC)

B5200   433   445   907   666   3844   3834   444   3804   3846

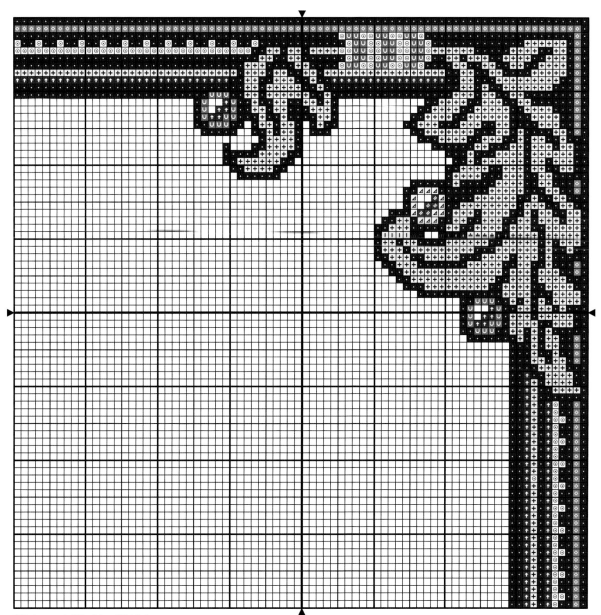

Stitch count: 80 wide x 80 high

WOODBLOCK LETTERS

Inspired by the time-battered beauty of carved wood-block lettering and illuminated initials, these letters can easily be updated with contemporary colours to give a modern style, or stitched in a muted palette for a more traditional look. This framed alphabet works well if creating longer word designs, as each letter can be butted up against another without spacing. For alternate threads see Thread Conversion Tables.

Stitch count: 80 wide x 80 high

Stitch count: 80 wide x 80 high

IDEA... Keep things simple and just stitch in two different colours – one for the letter and one for the background square.

Stranded cotton colours (DMC)

646   310   B5200

Stitch count: 80 wide x 80 high

Stranded cotton colours (DMC)

| 646 | 310 | B5200 |

Stitch count: 80 wide x 80 high

Stitch count: 80 wide x 80 high

Stranded cotton colours (DMC)

646   310   B5200

Stitch count: 80 wide x 80 high

Stitch count: 80 wide x 80 high

Stranded cotton colours (DMC)

646   310   B5200

Stitch count: 80 wide x 80 high

Stitch count: 80 wide x 80 high

Stranded cotton colours (DMC)

646   310   B5200

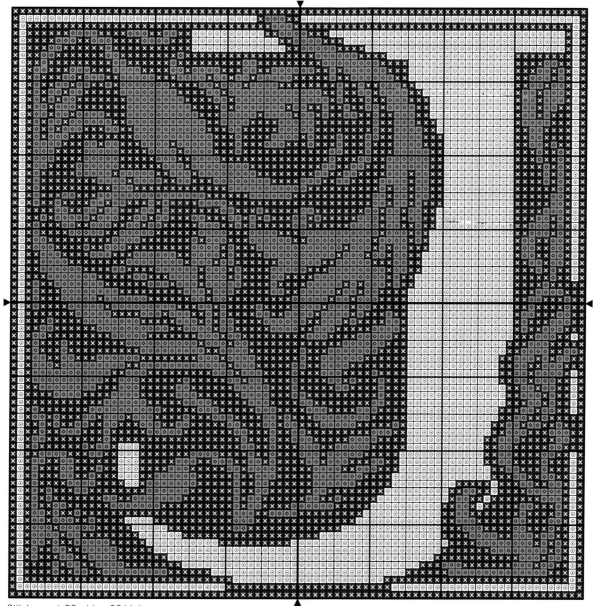

Stitch count: 80 wide x 80 high

Stitch count: 80 wide x 80 high

Stranded cotton colours (DMC)

646   310   B5200

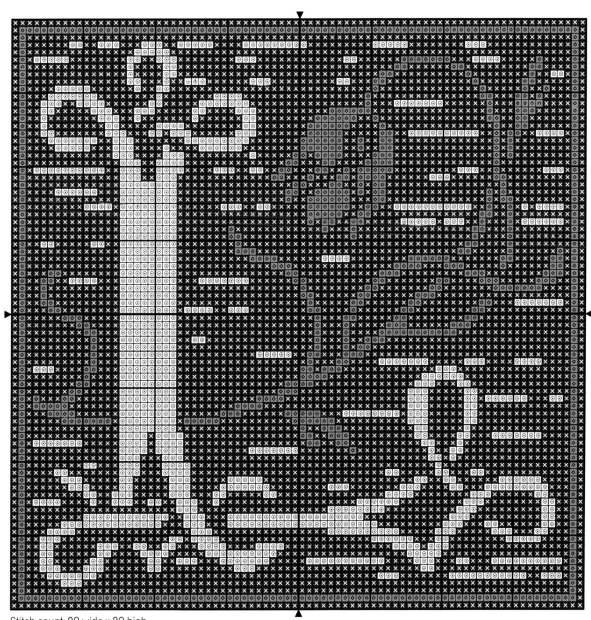

Stitch count: 80 wide x 80 high

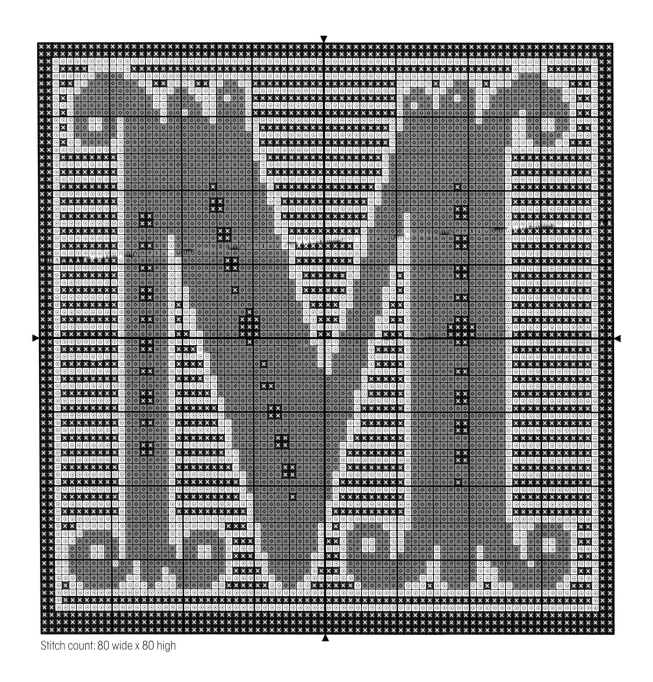

Stitch count: 80 wide x 80 high

Stranded cotton colours (DMC)

646   310   B5200

Stitch count: 80 wide x 80 high

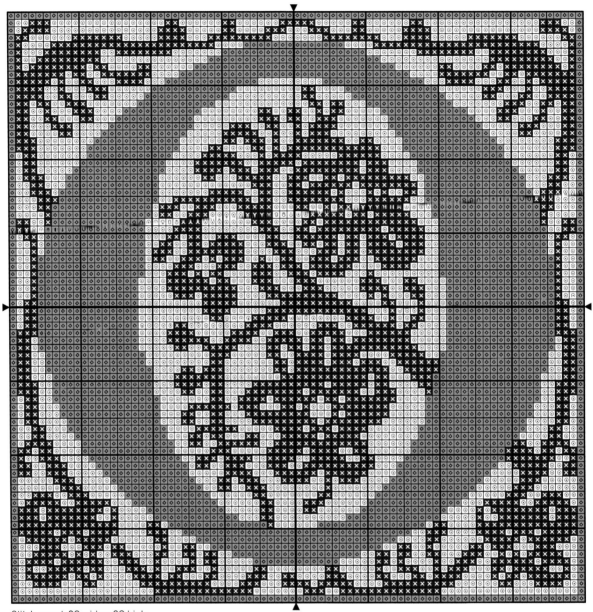

Stitch count: 80 wide x 80 high

Stranded cotton colours (DMC)

646   310   B5200

Stitch count: 80 wide x 80 high

Stitch count: 80 wide x 80 high

Stranded cotton colours (DMC)

646   310   B5200

Stitch count: 80 wide x 80 high

Stitch count: 80 wide x 80 high

Stranded cotton colours (DMC)

646   310   B5200

Stitch count: 80 wide x 80 high

IDEA... These letters are perfect for making alphabet blocks or alternatively, create a scaled-up version by adding a corner border and stitching on a large-gauge canvas to create a cube-shaped cushion or pouf.

Stitch count: 80 wide x 80 high

Stranded cotton colours (DMC)

646   310   B5200

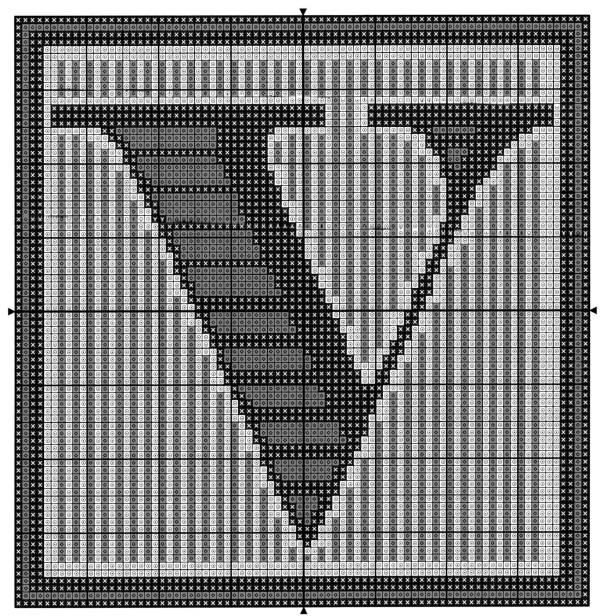

Stitch count: 80 wide x 80 high

Stitch count: 80 wide x 80 high

Stranded cotton colours (DMC)

646   310   B5200

Stitch count: 80 wide x 80 high

Stitch count: 80 wide x 80 high

Stranded cotton colours (DMC)

646   310   B5200

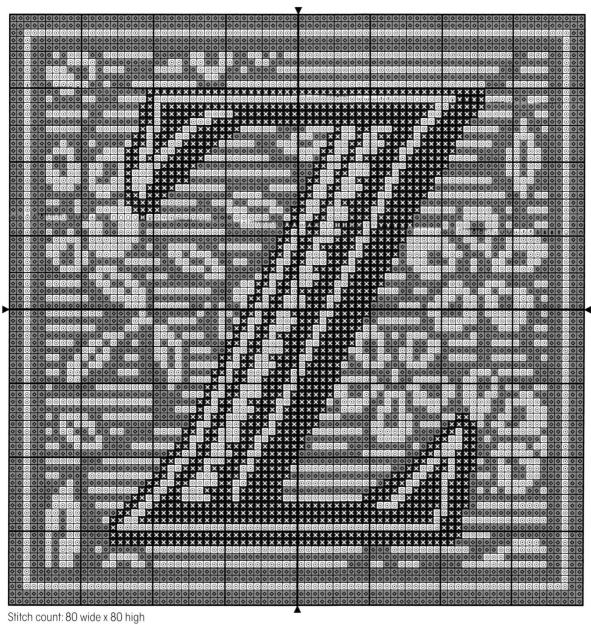

Stitch count: 80 wide x 80 high

Stitch count: 80 wide x 80 high

Stranded cotton colours (DMC)

646   310   B5200

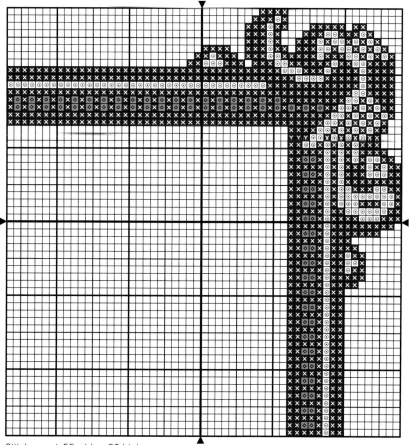

Stitch count: 55 wide x 58 high

Stitch count: 80 wide x 80 high

Stranded cotton colours (DMC)

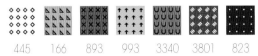

445   166   893   993   3340   3801   823

Stitch count: 80 wide x 80 high

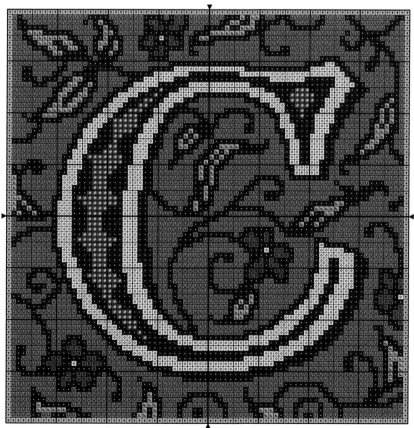

Stitch count: 80 wide x 80 high   Enlarge the charts by photocopying if desired

SHADOW LETTERS

These lovely letters work beautifully for sentiments or name designs. The modern outlined designs will add a retro feel to any project and are easy to stitch. Name cushions in a mix of bright colours work particularly well in this font, as the style reflects a bold poster design. Simply stitch the shadowed outline or fill with a contrasting colour for an even more striking look. For alternate threads see Thread Conversion Tables.

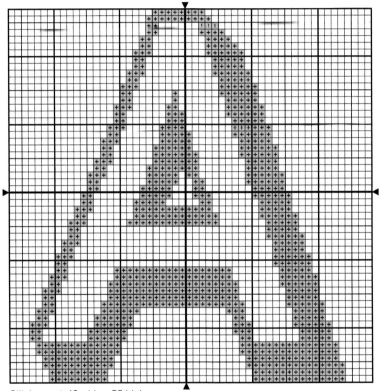

Stitch count: 48 wide x 55 high

IDEA... create a personal gift for a new baby by stitching the name in soft pastels and adding a floral border.

Stranded cotton colours (DMC)

| 3846 | 604 | 726 | 3824 | 307 |

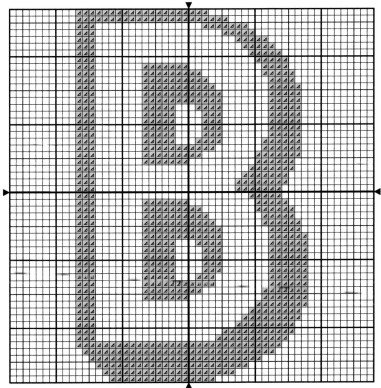

Stitch count: 35 wide x 55 high

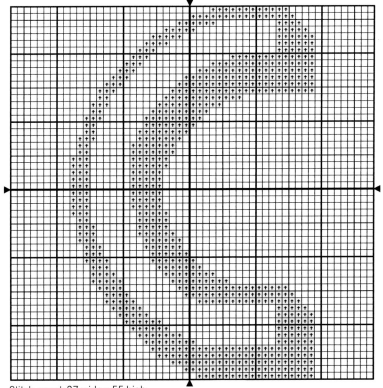

Stitch count: 37 wide x 55 high

Stranded cotton
colours (DMC)

3846

604

726

3824

307

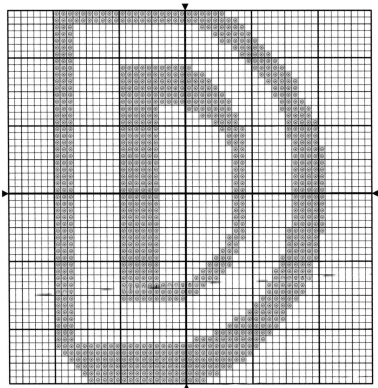

Stitch count: 41 wide x 55 high

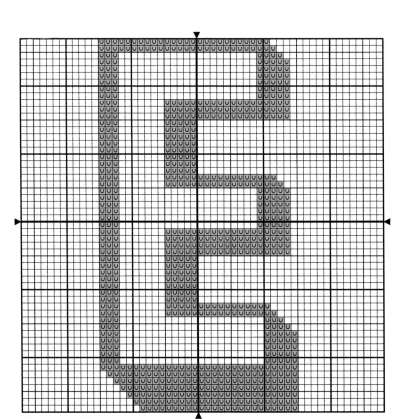

Stitch count: 30 wide x 55 high

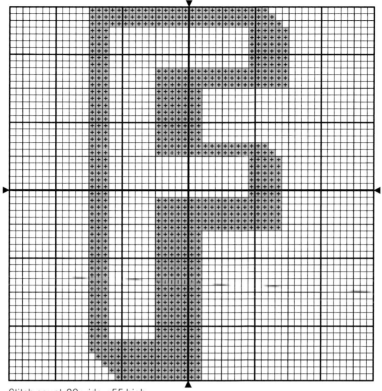

Stitch count: 29 wide x 55 high

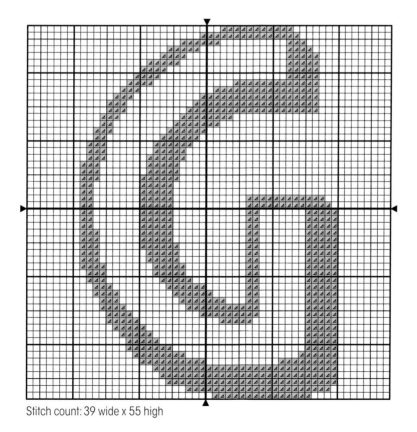

Stitch count: 39 wide x 55 high

Stranded cotton
colours (DMC)

3846

604

726

3824

307

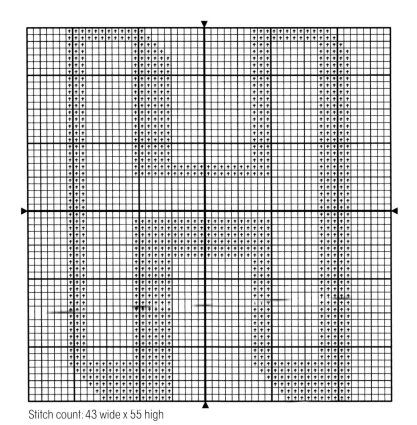

Stitch count: 43 wide x 55 high

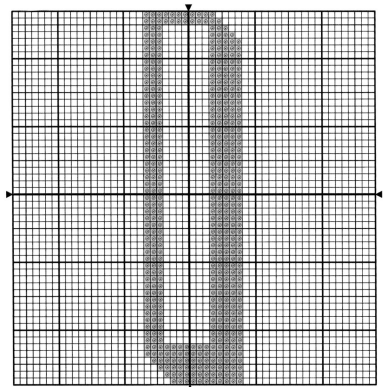

Stitch count: 15 wide x 55 high

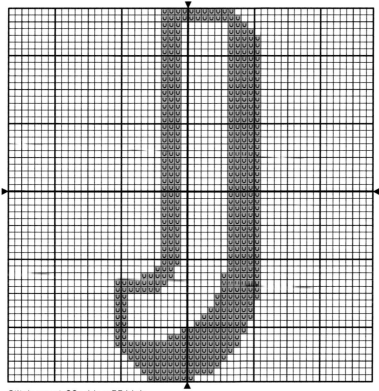

Stitch count: 22 wide x 55 high

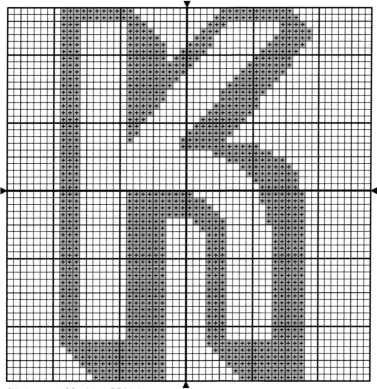

Stitch count: 38 wide x 55 high

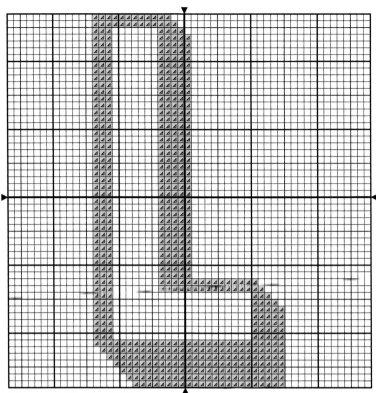

Stranded cotton
colours (DMC)

3846

604

726

3824

307

Stitch count: 29 wide x 55 high

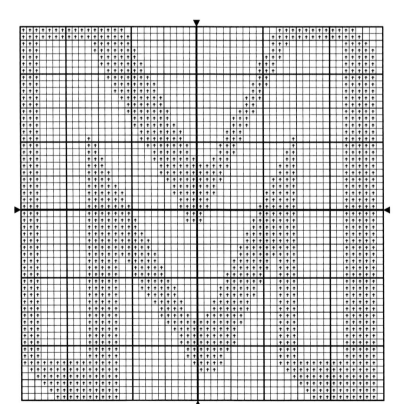

Stitch count: 54 wide x 55 high

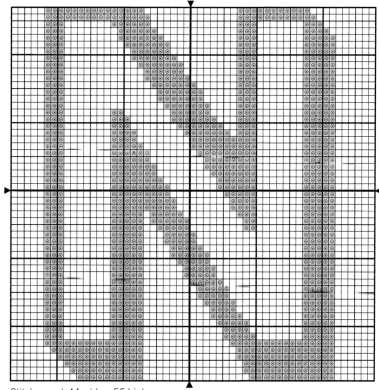

Stitch count: 44 wide x 55 high

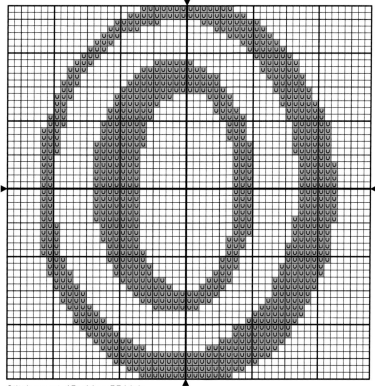

Stitch count: 45 wide x 55 high

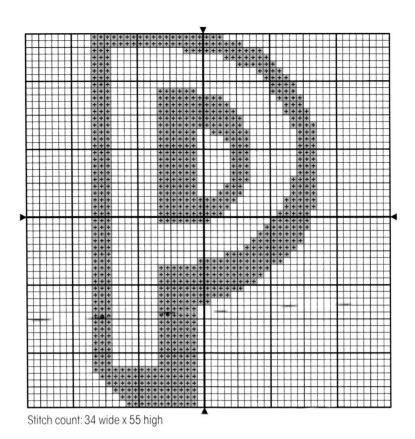

Stitch count: 34 wide x 55 high

Stranded cotton colours (DMC)

▲▲▲▲	3846
++++	604
⊚⊚⊚⊚	726
∪∪∪∪	3824
↑↑↑↑	307

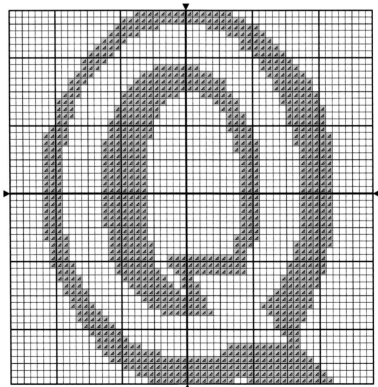

Stitch count: 44 wide x 55 high

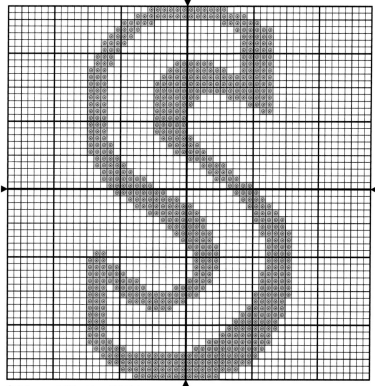

Stitch count: 36 wide x 55 high

Stitch count: 31 wide x 55 high

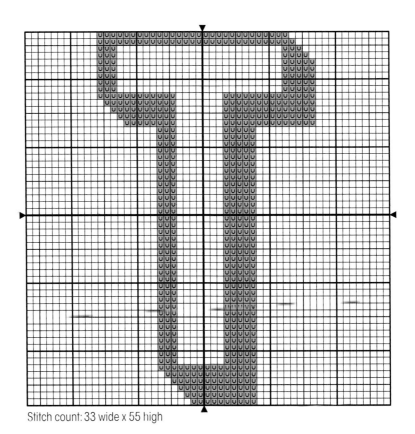

Stranded cotton
colours (DMC)

▰▰▰▰
▰▰▰▰ 3846
▰▰▰▰

✛✛✛✛
✛✛✛✛ 604
✛✛✛✛

◉◉◉◉
◉◉◉◉ 726
◉◉◉◉

ᴜᴜᴜᴜ
ᴜᴜᴜᴜ 3824
ᴜᴜᴜᴜ

↑↑↑↑↑
↑↑↑↑↑ 307
↑↑↑↑↑

Stitch count: 33 wide x 55 high

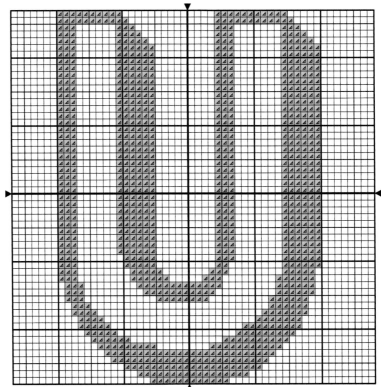

Stitch count: 40 wide x 55 high

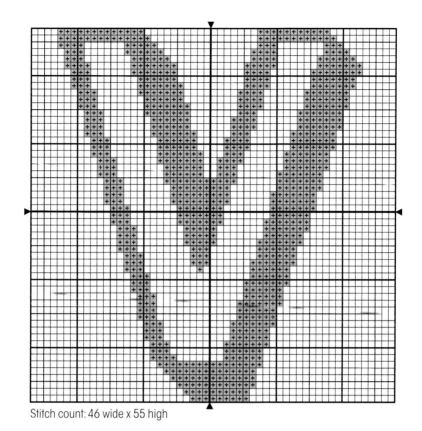

Stitch count: 46 wide x 55 high

Stitch count: 64 wide x 55 high

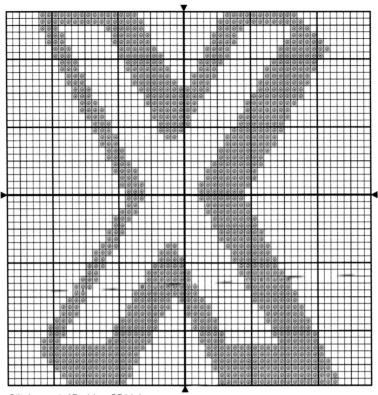

Stranded cotton
colours (DMC)

▲▲▲▲ 3846
++++ 604
⊚⊚⊚⊚ 726
UUUU 3824
↑↑↑↑ 307

Stitch count: 45 wide x 55 high

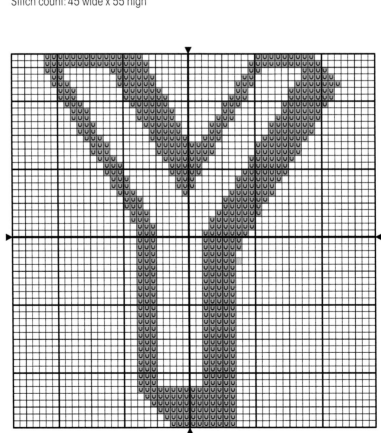

Stitch count: 45 wide x 55 high

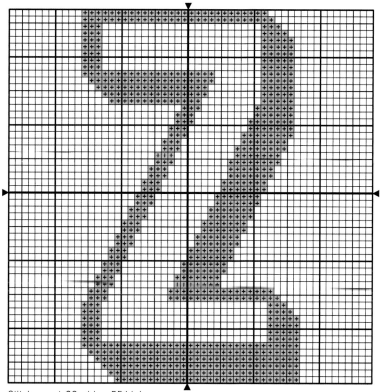

Stitch count: 33 wide x 55 high

IDEA... These letters work well together or can be mixed with the other fonts in this book to create larger samplers and phrases – just stitch each word in the different styles to create a fashionably eclectic picture or cushion.

IDEA... For a simpler look try stitching just the outside row of stitches on the face of each letter to create an outlined font.

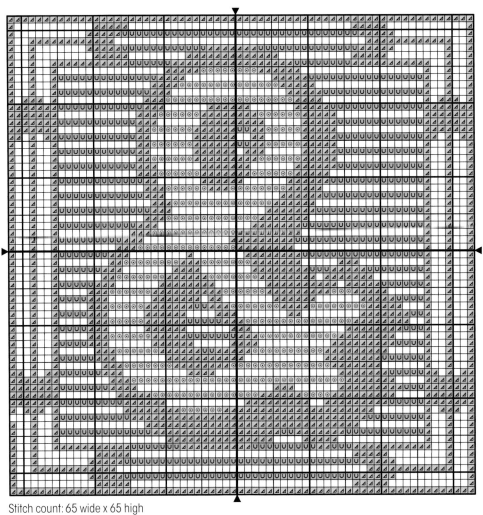

Stitch count: 65 wide x 65 high

Stranded cotton colours (DMC)

3846   604   726   3824   307

IDEA...   For a fun circus-themed font
try filling each blank letter
with multicoloured stripes in
varying directions.

Stitch count: 93 wide x 93 high

SCREEN-PRINT NUMBERS

Emulating the grainy, textured look of layered screen-printed type, these numbers will add a poster-style quality to any personal number or date. Designed using retro fonts, the bold elements are simple and quick to stitch and are perfect for beginners to create fast, fun projects. These bold, boisterous designs are great for a little boy's room or grown-up boy's office! For alternate threads see Thread Conversion Tables.

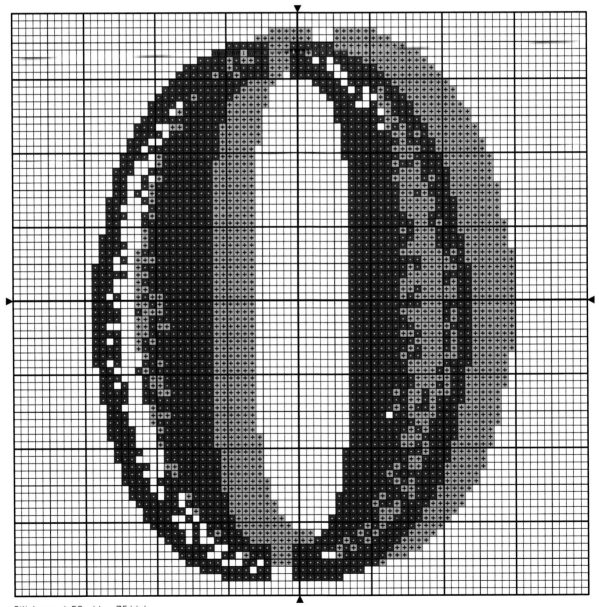

Stitch count: 59 wide x 75 high

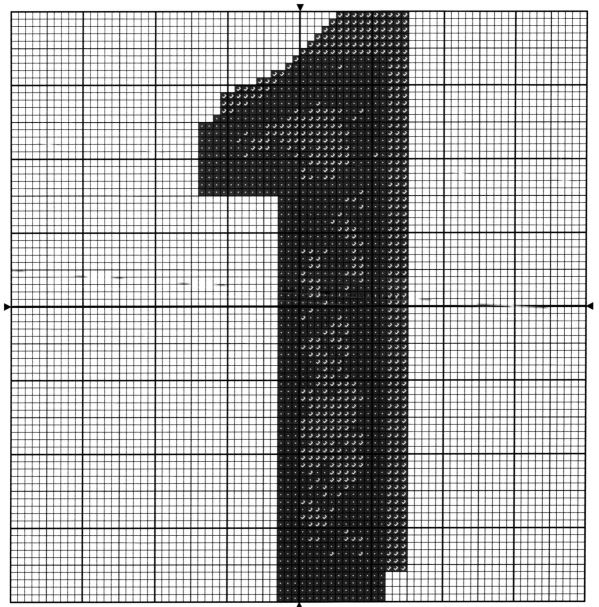

Stitch count: 29 wide x 80 high

IDEA... Stitch numbers 1-10 in a row for a modern take on a 'learn to count' number banner for a child's bedroom.

Stranded cotton colours (DMC)

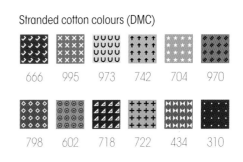

666 995 973 742 704 970

798 602 718 722 434 310

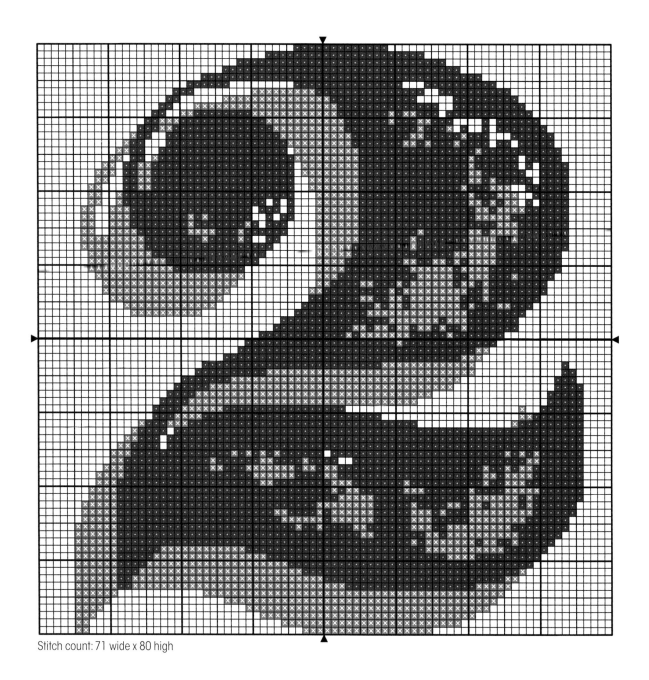

Stitch count: 71 wide x 80 high

Stranded cotton colours (DMC)

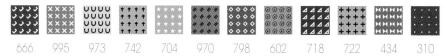

666   995   973   742   704   970   798   602   718   722   434   310

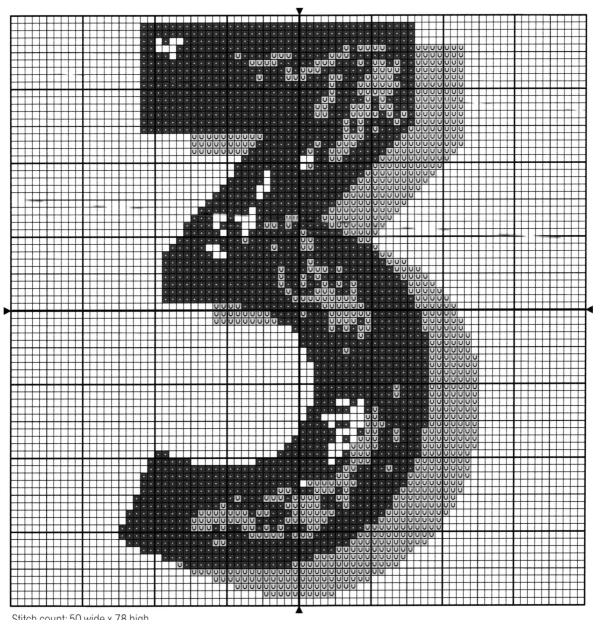

Stitch count: 50 wide x 78 high

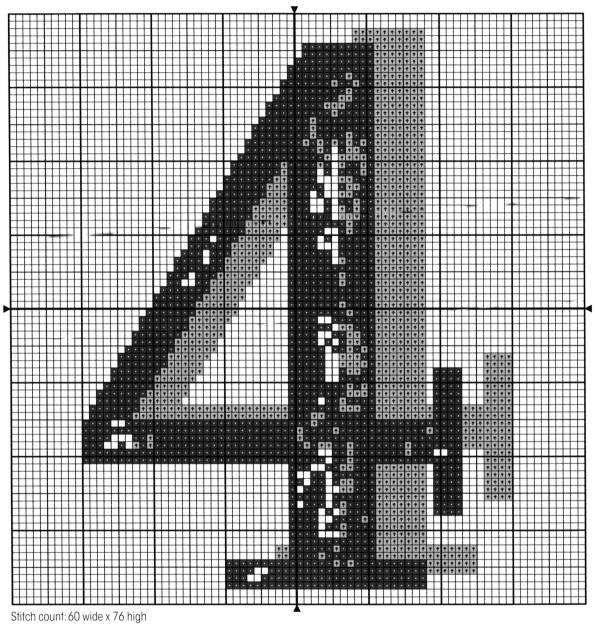

Stitch count: 60 wide x 76 high

Stranded cotton colours (DMC)

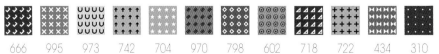

666   995   973   742   704   970   798   602   718   722   434   310

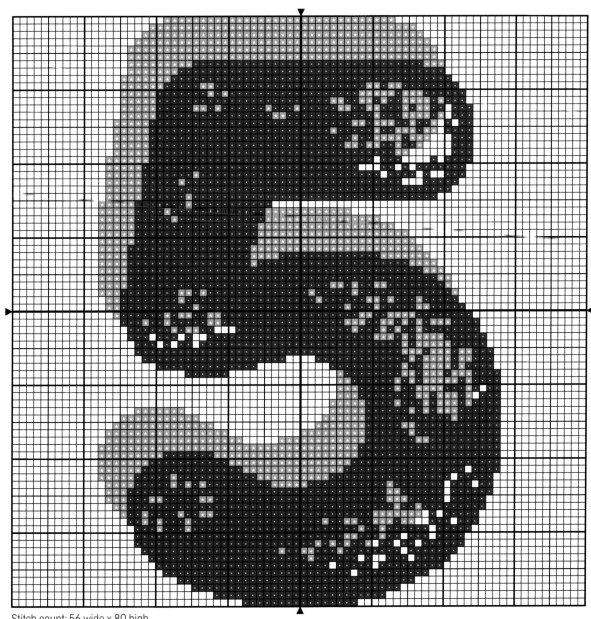

Stitch count: 56 wide x 80 high

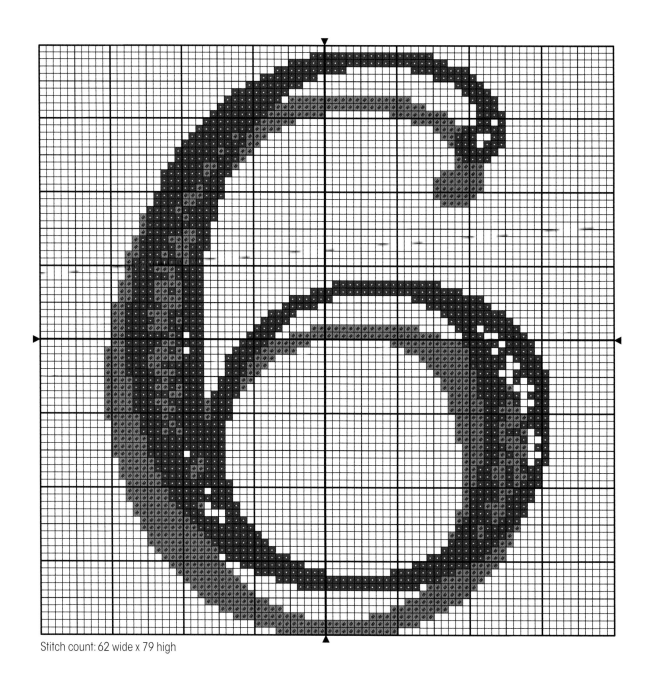

Stitch count: 62 wide x 79 high

Stranded cotton colours (DMC)

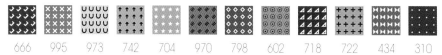

666   995   973   742   704   970   798   602   718   722   434   310

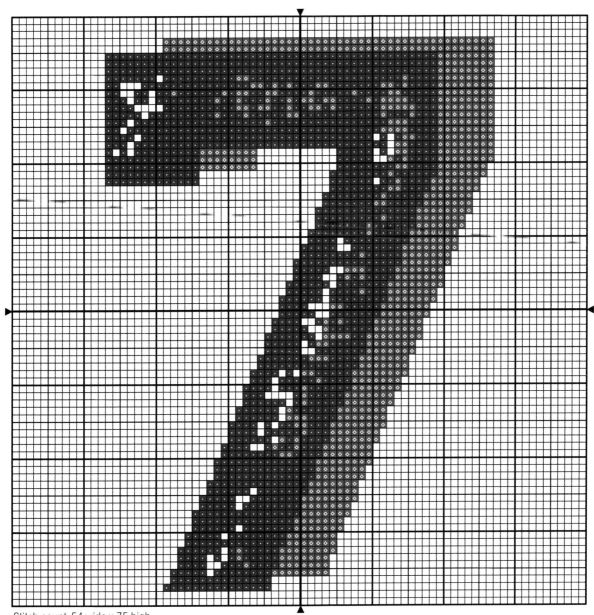

Stitch count: 54 wide x 75 high

IDEA... Add a masculine edge by stitching the numbers in dark navy and shades of blue and grey. Finish by simply stretching over a canvas.

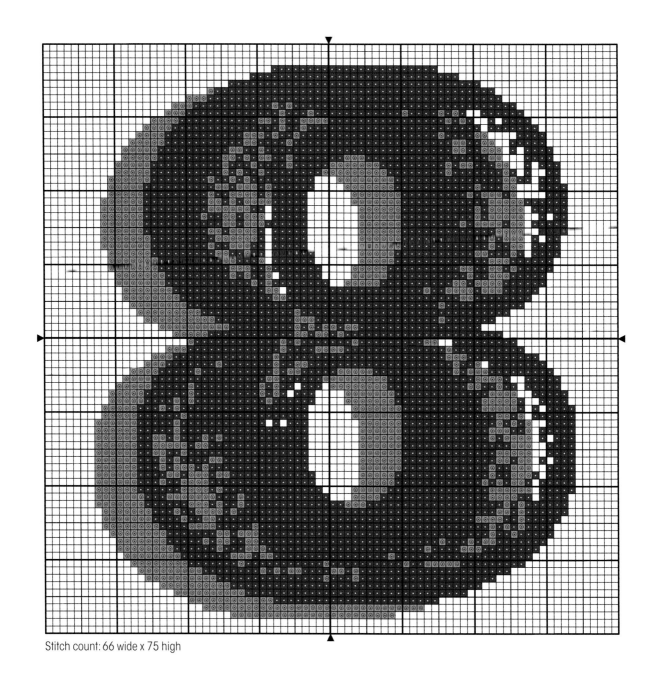

Stitch count: 66 wide x 75 high

Stranded cotton colours (DMC)

666   995   973   742   704   970   798   602   718   722   434   310

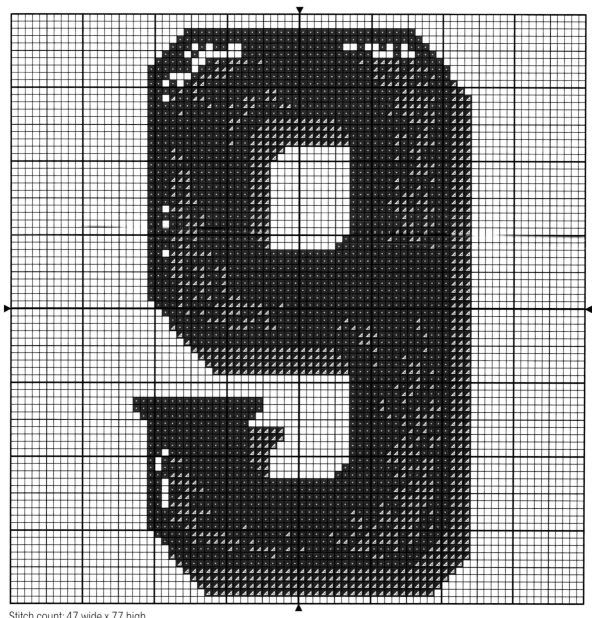

Stitch count: 47 wide x 77 high

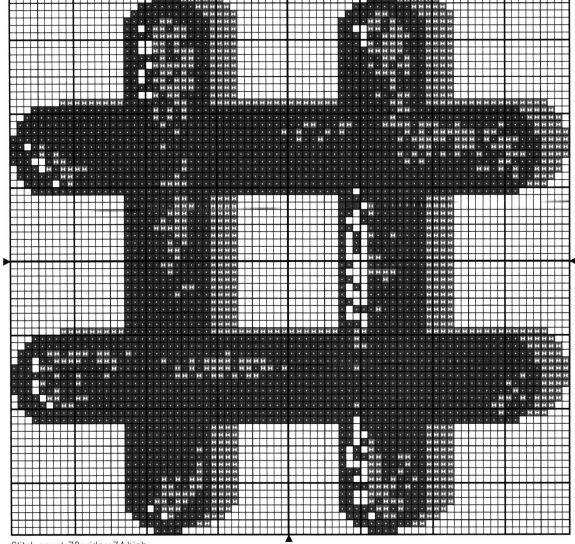

Stitch count: 78 wide x 74 high

Stranded cotton colours (DMC)

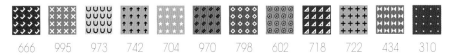

666   995   973   742   704   970   798   602   718   722   434   310

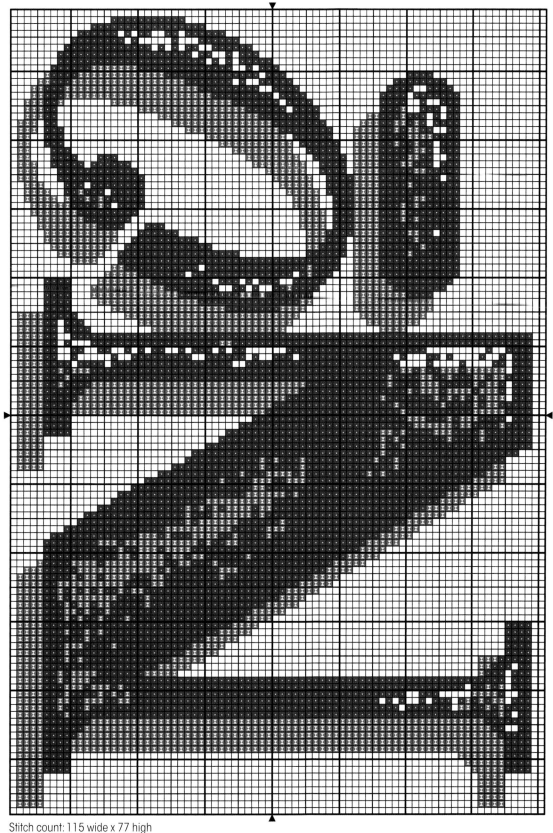

Stitch count: 115 wide x 77 high

VINTAGE NUMBERS

With its fresh Scandinavian-inspired style, the smaller size of these vintage numbers is perfect for stitching a memorable date cushion. Use contemporary clashing colours to up the wow factor, or calm things down with soft earthy tones for a more rustic look. Thanks to the combination of Art Deco numerals and Scandinavian simplicity, the floral cut-outs add a dainty feature, whilst the linear shadow effect gives them a modern, graphic edge. For alternate threads see Thread Conversion Tables.

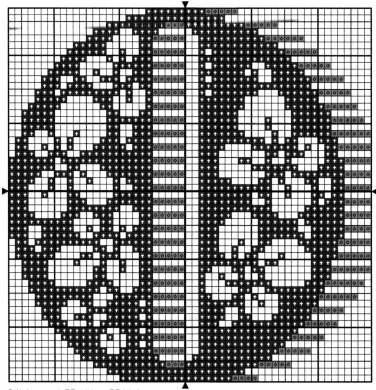

Stitch count: 55 wide x 55 high

IDEA... Try adding a sparkly embellishment to a cushion by stitching the shadow lines in a gold metallic thread.

Stranded cotton colours (DMC)

798   608

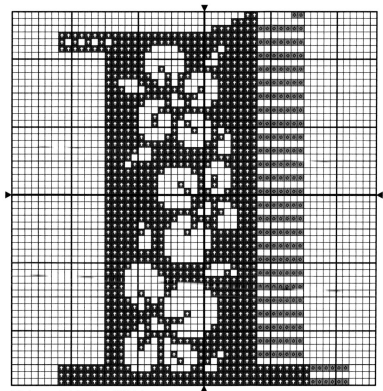

Stitch count: 44 wide x 55 high

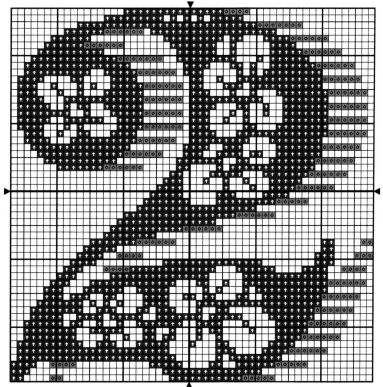

Stitch count: 55 wide x 55 high

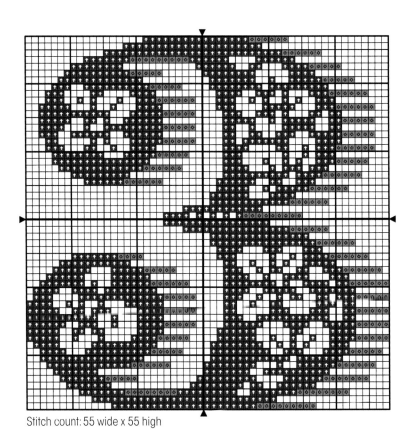

Stranded cotton
colours (DMC)

 798

 608

Stitch count: 55 wide x 55 high

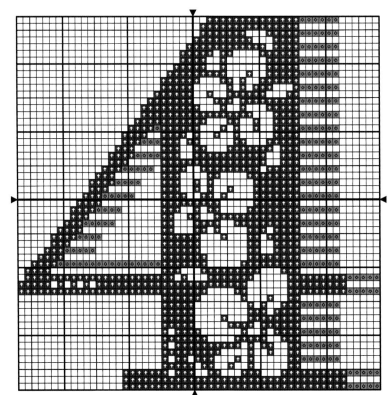

Stitch count: 55 wide x 55 high

Stitch count: 55 wide x 55 high

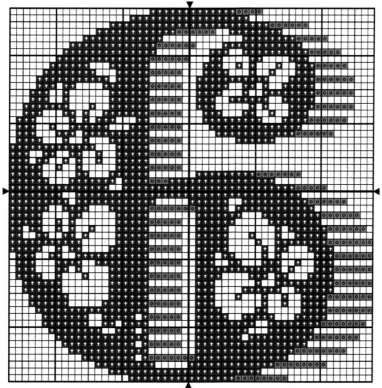

Stitch count: 55 wide x 55 high

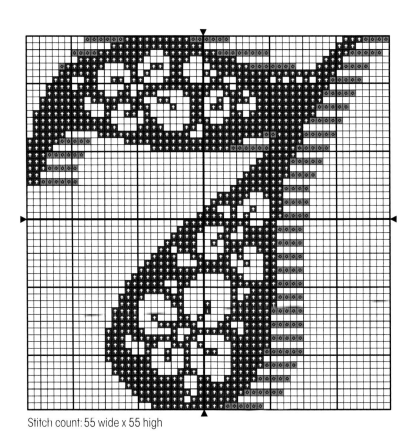

Stranded cotton
colours (DMC)

 798

 608

Stitch count: 55 wide x 55 high

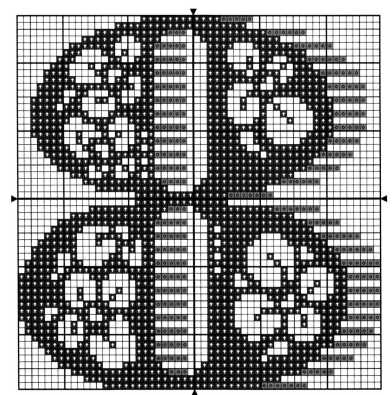

Stitch count: 55 wide x 55 high

Stitch count: 55 wide x 55 high

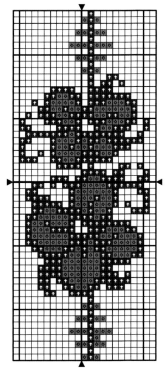

Stitch count: 21 wide x 55 high

113

FLORAL NUMBERS

Echoing the plant-like contours of Art Nouveau decoration, these numbers have an organic feel mixed with the playfulness of ditsy florals. Add warmth and colour to your home by stitching the leaves and flowers in a vibrant Mediterranean palette. The bold turquoise and bright pastels harmonize with a dark background fabric and really make the numbers stand out. For alternate threads see Thread Conversion Tables.

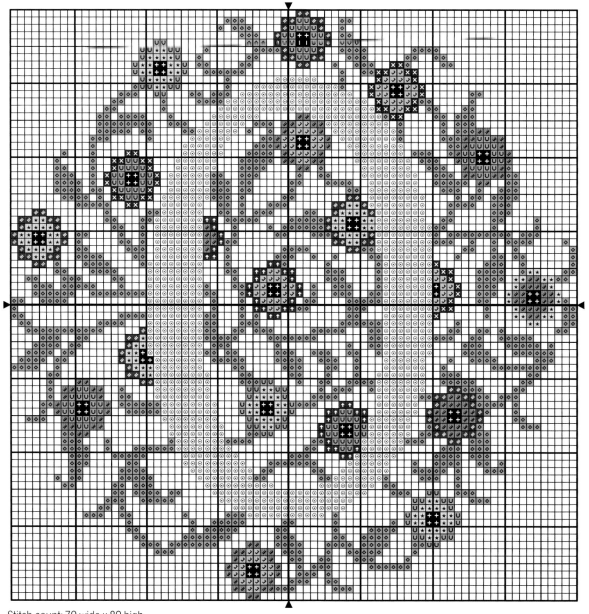

Stitch count: 79 wide x 80 high

Stitch count: 79 wide x 80 high

IDEA... For a more vintage, French feel, stitch on a dark linen in simple pale creams, beiges and white thread.

Stranded cotton colours (DMC)

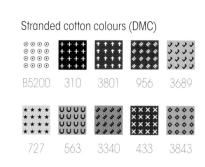

B5200	310	3801	956	3689
727	563	3340	433	3843

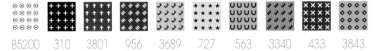

Stitch count: 79 wide x 80 high

Stranded cotton colours (DMC)

B5200	310	3801	956	3689	727	563	3340	433	3843

Stitch count: 79 wide x 80 high

Stitch count: 79 wide x 80 high

Stranded cotton colours (DMC)

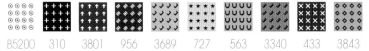

B5200   310   3801   956   3689   727   563   3340   433   3843

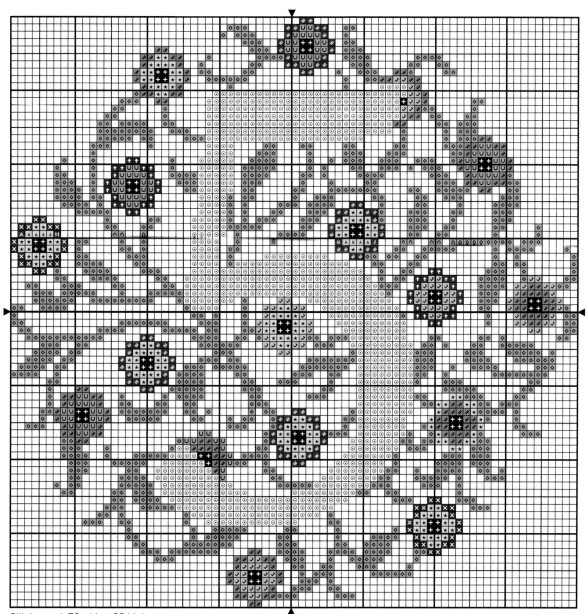

Stitch count: 79 wide x 80 high

IDEA... Infuse a touch of eclectic quirkiness to your interiors by mixing these numbers with lots of other floral fabrics. The circular shapes lend themselves to framing in circular embroidery hoops.

Stitch count: 79 wide x 80 high

Stranded cotton colours (DMC)

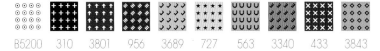

B5200   310   3801   956   3689   727   563   3340   433   3843

Stitch count: 79 wide x 80 high

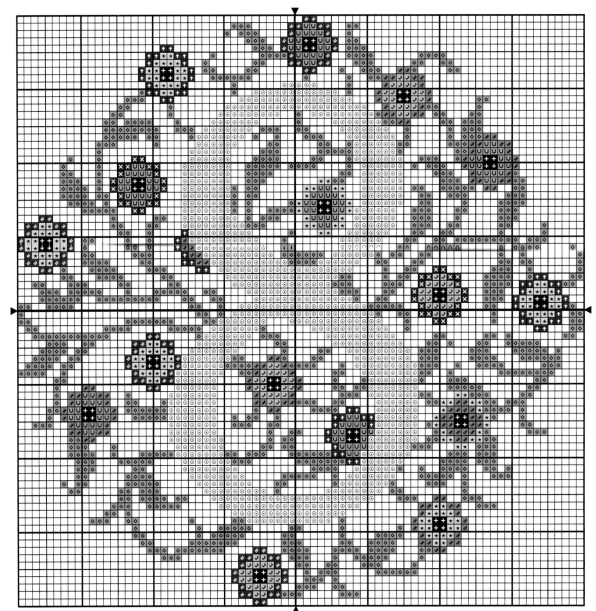

Stitch count: 79 wide x 80 high

Stranded cotton colours (DMC)

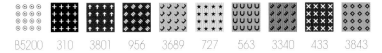

| B5200 | 310 | 3801 | 956 | 3689 | 727 | 563 | 3340 | 433 | 3843 |

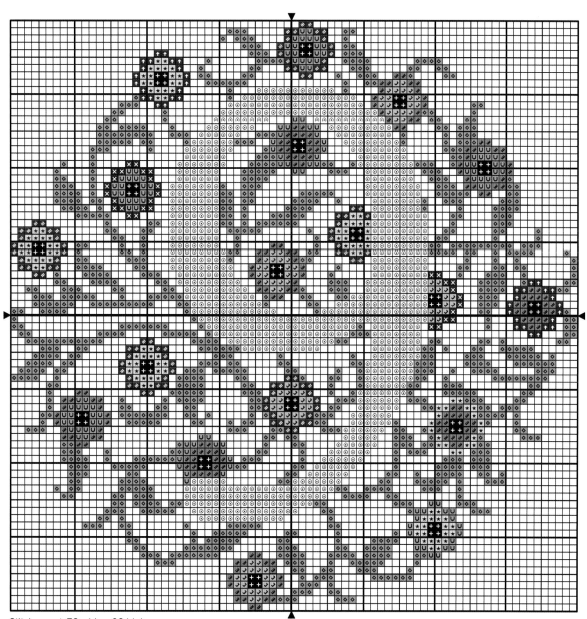

Stitch count: 79 wide x 80 high

IDEA... These designs make perfect table
number markers for a wedding – just
stitch in your chosen colours for a
lovely reminder of the day. Use them
afterwards to display the date of the
wedding on your bedroom wall.

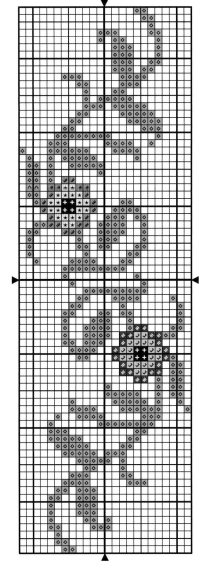

Stitch count: 24 wide x 74 high

Stranded cotton colours (DMC)

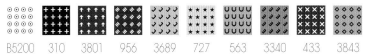

B5200   310   3801   956   3689   727   563   3340   433   3843

THREAD CONVERSION TABLES

CIRCUS LETTERS

Colour	DMC	DMC TAPESTRY	ANCHOR	ANCHOR TAPESTRY	APPLETONS
White	B5200	BLANC	1	8000	991B
Brown	433	7479	358	9452	305
Yellow	445	7431	288	8114	551
Green	907	7342	255	9156	253
Red	666	7666	335	8200	446
Turquoise	3844	7995	410	8808	485
Purple	3834	7017	100	8530	895
Lime Yellow	444	7433	291	8094	997
Pink	3804	7603	63	8456	946
Light Blue	3846	7036	1090	8804	481

WOODBLOCK LETTERS

Colour	DMC	DMC TAPESTRY	ANCHOR	ANCHOR TAPESTRY	APPLETONS
Grey	646	7285	8581	8718	964
Black	310	NOIR	403	9800	993
White	B5200	BLANC	1	8000	991B

SHADOW LETTERS

Colour	DMC	DMC TAPESTRY	ANCHOR	ANCHOR TAPESTRY	APPLETONS
Turquoise	3846	7036	1090	8804	481
Pink	604	7133	55	8414	941
Light Orange	726	7971	295	8120	472
Peach	3824	7851	8	8258	854
Yellow	307	7433	289	8094	551

SCREEN-PRINT NUMBERS

Colour	DMC	DMC TAPESTRY	ANCHOR	ANCHOR TAPESTRY	APPLETONS
Red	666	7544	46	8024	447
Blue	995	7995	410	8808	464
Yellow	973	7726	297	8118	553
Light Orange	742	7971	303	8120	474
Green	704	7341	256	91154	425
Dark Orange	970	7740	316	8156	557
Peacock Blue	798	7797	131	8690	895
Pink	602	7804	63	8454	944
Magenta	718	7157	88	8492	804
Peach	722	7214	323	8232	854
Brown	434	7845	310	9448	302
Black	310	NOIR	403	9800	933

VINTAGE NUMBERS

Colour	DMC	DMC TAPESTRY	ANCHOR	ANCHOR TAPESTRY	APPLETONS
Blue	798	7317	146	8630	464
Orange	608	7946	330	8194	442

FLORAL NUMBERS

Colour	DMC	DMC TAPESTRY	ANCHOR	ANCHOR TAPESTRY	APPLETONS
White	B5200	BLANC	1	8000	991B
Black	310	NOIR	403	9800	993
Red	3801	7640	1098	8440	502
Pink	956	7903	40	8456	946
Light Pink	3689	7151	49	8484	751
Yellow	727	7431	293	8114	551
Mint Green	563	7598	208	8934	523
Peach	3340	7851	329	8258	622
Brown	433	7479	358	8106	305
Turquoise	3843	7037	1089	8806	484

ABOUT THE AUTHOR

I have always been creative – I can't remember ever being interested in anything else! When I was a child I was always drawing or making things, from stuffed toys to cross-stitched samplers. I designed my first needlepoint over twenty years ago, age ten, when I asked my mother to stitch a sun and moon cushion that I had sketched on a scrap of squared paper. As a result it was inevitable that

I went on to study textiles and fine art painting (my other passion!) at college and university. I then started my journey in needlepoint design in 2009. After working for a hand-painted needlepoint company in London and freelancing for a number of craft magazines, including *Cross Stitcher* magazine, I realised there was a gap in the market for printed needlepoint kits that had a contemporary edge and that would also be interesting to stitch, so I decided to be brave and go it alone, I developed my own range of designs and set up my website www.felicityhall.co.uk and never looked back!

ACKNOWLEDGMENTS

Thank you very much to all the team at David & Charles, especially Sarah Callard, Jeni Hennah, Matt Hutchings, Jenny Stanley and Lin Clements. A big thank you to my mum, Christine Hall, for helping to stitch some of the project samples, and for always being so encouraging and inspiring. And lastly, thank you to my husband Dave, who is so supportive and endlessly puts up with mountains of wool and needles left in the arms of the sofa!

SUPPLIERS

NEEDLES & THREADERS
www.jjneedles.com

THREADS
www.appletons.org.uk
Includes a list of shops and online stockists of Appletons wool

www.dmccreative.co.uk
DMC threads, fabrics and accessories

www.coatscrafts.co.uk
Anchor threads, fabrics and accessories

FABRIC & CANVAS
www.zweigartfabric.com
The best needlework fabric you can buy. Includes a list of stockists

DAYLIGHT LAMPS
www.daylightcompany.com
For daylight lamps, magnifiers and accessories for needlework

FRAMES & HOOPS
www.elbesee.co.uk

TRIMS
www.macculloch-wallis.co.uk
Great selection of trims, zips, fabrics and embellishments

www.vvrouleaux.com
Fantastic selection of ribbon, trims and embellishments

CUSHION PADS
www.merrick-day.com

GENERAL STITCHING ACCESSORIES, FABRICS & THREADS
www.sewandso.co.uk
www.sewexciting.co.uk
www.liberty.co.uk

INDEX

PROJECT MATERIALS

The following materials were used to create
the projects on pages 16-21.

WOODBLOCK ALPHABET BLOCKS

Stitched using six strands of Anchor stranded
cotton on 14 hpi Darice plastic canvas.

CIRCUS 'A' CUSHION

Stitched using one strand of Appletons 4-ply Tapestry
wool on 10 hpi Zweigart white interlock canvas.

WOODBLOCK 'Z' PICTURE

Stitched using one strand of Appletons 4-ply Tapestry
wool on 10 hpi Zweigart white interlock canvas.

FLORAL TABLE NUMBERS

Stitched using one strand of DMC stranded cotton
on 16 hpi Zweigart Black and White Aida.

SHADOW ALPHABET NAME CANVAS

Stitched using Anchor Pearl Cotton No.8,
on 14 hpi Zweigart white Aida.

INITIAL EMBROIDERY HOOPS

Stitched using one strand of Anchor Pearl cotton No.8 on 14
hpi Zweigart Vintage Country Mocha (reverse side) Aida.

VINTAGE DATE CUSHION

Stitched using one strand of DMC Pearl cotton No.5
on 20 hpi Zweigart Bellana Marble Evenweave.

A DAVID & CHARLES BOOK
© F&W Media International, Ltd 2014

David & Charles is an imprint of F&W Media International, Ltd
Brunel House, Forde Close, Newton Abbot, TQ12 4PU, UK

F&W Media International, Ltd is a subsidiary of F+W Media, Inc
10151 Carver Road, Suite #200, Blue Ash, OH 45242, USA

Text and Designs © Felicity Hall 2014
Layout and Photography © F&W Media International, Ltd 2014

First published in the UK and USA in 2014

Names of manufacturers and product ranges are provided for
the information of readers, with no intention to infringe copyright
or trademarks.

A catalogue record for this book is available from the British Library.

ISBN-13: 978-1-4463-0391-7
ISBN-10: 1-4463-0391-8

Printed in China by RR Donnelley for:
F&W Media International, Ltd
Brunel House, Forde Close, Newton Abbot, TQ12 4PU, UK

10 9 8 7 6 5 4 3 2 1

Acquisitions Editor: Jeni Hennah
Desk Editor: Matthew Hutchings
Project Editor: Linda Clements
Designer: Jennifer Stanley
Photographer: Jennifer Stanley, Jack Kirby and Jack Gorman
Senior Production Controller: Kelly Smith

F+W Media publishes high quality books on a wide range of
subjects. For more great book ideas visit:
www.stitchcraftcreate.co.uk

LONDON COLLEGE OF MUSIC EXAMINATIONS

Step Two

Classical
Guitar Playing

Compiled by
Tony Skinner, Raymond Burley and Amanda Cook
on behalf of

The Specialists in Guitar Education

RGT ®

Registry of Guitar Tutors

Printed in the EU

ONLINE PRINTED BY

A CIP record for this publication is available from the British Library
ISBN: 978-1-905908-20-2

Published by Registry Publications

Registry Mews, Wilton Rd, Bexhill, Sussex, TN40 1HY

Cover artwork by Danielle Croft. Design by JAK Images.

Compiled for LCM Exams by

www.RGT.org

v.20150210

INTRODUCTION _____

This publication is part of a progressive series of ten handbooks, primarily intended for candidates considering taking the London College Of Music examinations in classical guitar playing. However, given each handbook's wide content of musical repertoire and associated educational material, the series provides a solid foundation of musical education for any classical guitar student – whether intending to take an examination or not. Whilst the handbooks can be used for independent study, they are ideally intended as a supplement to individual or group tuition.

Examination entry

An examination entry form is provided at the rear of each handbook. This is the only valid entry form for the London College Of Music classical guitar examinations. Please note that *if the entry form is detached and lost, it will not be replaced under any circumstances* and the candidate will be required to obtain a replacement handbook to obtain another entry form. For candidates making online entries for classical guitar examinations, the handbook entry form must still be completed and must bo submitted by post before the entry deadline to:

UK and Ireland entries: LCM Exams, University of West London, St Mary's Road, Ealing, London, W5 5RF, UK.

Entries not from the UK and Ireland: the completed entry form should be sent to your local LCM Exams Representative.

Editorial information

Examination performances must be from this handbook edition. All performance pieces should be played in full, including all repeats shown; the pieces have been edited specifically for examination use, with all non-required repeat markings omitted.

Tempos, fingering and dynamic markings are for general guidance only and need not be rigidly adhered to, providing an effective musical result is achieved.

Pick-hand fingering is normally shown on the stem side of the notes:
p = thumb; *i* = index finger; *m* = middle finger; *a* = third finger.

Fret-hand fingering is shown with the numbers 1 2 3 4, normally to the left of the notehead.
0 indicates an open string.

String numbers are shown in a circle, normally below the note. For example, ⑥ = 6th string.

TECHNICAL WORK _____

The examiner will select some of the scales and chords shown below and ask the candidate to play them from memory. To allow for flexibility in teaching approaches, the fingering suggestions given below are not compulsory and alternative systematic fingerings, that are musically effective, will be accepted. Suggested tempos are for general guidance only; slightly slower or faster performances will be acceptable, providing that the tempo is evenly maintained.

A maximum of 25 marks may be awarded in this section of the examination. Overall, the examiner will be listening for accurate, even and clear playing.

Scales

Scales should be played ascending and descending, i.e. from the lowest note to the highest and back again, without a pause and without repeating the top note. Suggested fret-hand fingering is provided with the notation below. It is recommended that scales are picked using alternating *i* and *m* fingering. Either tirando (free stroke) or apoyando (rest stroke) can be used.

At this level, scales should be played at an appropriate tempo of 112 beats per minute.

C major scale – 1 octave   **G major scale – 1 octave**

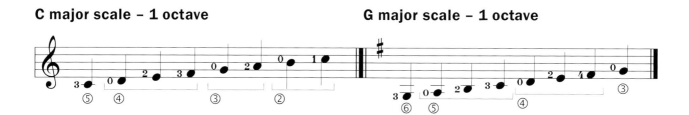

A harmonic minor scale – 1 octave   **E harmonic minor scale – 1 octave**

Chords

Chords should be played ascending only, and sounded string by string, starting with the lowest (root) note. To achieve a legato (i.e. smooth and over-ringing) sound, the whole chord shape should be fretted and kept on during playing. Chords should be played tirando, i.e. using free strokes. The recommended pick-hand fingering is *p* (thumb) for all bass strings, followed by *i m a* on the treble strings.

Chords should be played at an appropriate tempo of 152 beats per minute.

C major chord   **G major chord**   **A minor chord**   **E minor chord**

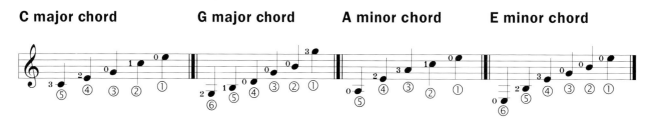

PERFORMANCE _____

Candidates should play any *two* melodies from Group A, plus any *one* piece from Group B. A maximum of 60 marks may be awarded in this section of the examination – i.e. up to 20 marks for each performance. Tempo markings are for general guidance only and do not need to be adhered to strictly. All repeat markings should be followed.

Performance Tips

Melodies:

- The melodies are all in the key of G major. This means that the notes contained in the melodies will all be taken from the G major scale, shown in the *Technical Work* section of this handbook; the only exceptions being some notes that, whilst still within the key, are just beyond the range of the one octave scale. It would be helpful preparation to thoroughly study the G major scale before starting to play any of these melodies.

- Suggestions for fingering are given in the first few bars of each melody and after that only where necessary.

- The first three melodies all include *first and second time endings*: the bars with a number 1 bracket above them should be omitted on the repeat playing and replaced with those starting below the number 2 bracket.

- *Spring* should be performed with a confident approach to evoke the bright mood of the music. The Bach *Minuet* has a dance-like character that requires an even tempo. *La Ci Darem La Mano* is an arrangement of a vocal duet from Mozart's opera *Don Giovanni* and the melody can be played in a lyrical way. The *William Tell* theme needs to be played at a brisk tempo in order to capture the lively spirit of the piece.

Malagueña:

- Don't be put off by the difficult-looking chords in the first two bars: both chords require only two fretted notes. Once you have learnt the chord shapes, they'll prove very useful – particularly as the first chord shape (E major) occurs many times throughout the piece as a 'spread chord', such as in bars 5 and 15.

- Be careful not to rush the first few bars, or you'll find it very difficult to maintain the tempo once the quaver (eighth note) section begins from bar 15.

- In bars 15 to 22, the melody lies in the bass and should be played throughout with the thumb. The repeated open high E string is there just to give a sense of movement and contrast; it should not be played too loudly.

- The key signature is A minor, although in this typical Spanish style the harmonic emphasis is on the dominant chord (E major).

The Chase:

- Throughout this piece the melody is played on the bass strings with the thumb. The open high E string notes that occur are included purely for rhythmic effect and to add to the sense of movement within the piece.

- The key signature is A minor.

- The first 16 bars are marked to be played first loudly and then softly when they are repeated.

- At the end of bar 32 the *D.C. al Fine* sign indicates that you should repeat from the beginning until the *Fine* (ending) sign at the end of bar 16. There is no need to repeat the first 16 bars again.

In A Rush:

- This piece should be performed at a fluent and regular tempo to capture its sense of momentum and excitement.

- Observe the changes in dynamics, including the accented notes in bars 7 and 8, and the crescendo (gradual increase in volume) in bar 11.

- Repeat dots show that the first 8 bars should be repeated.

- The key signature is C major.

Tension In The Air:

- This piece begins with a slow bassline played over a repeated treble-string pattern consisting of alternation between the top two open strings. The first four bars should be repeated.

- As the title suggests, the music should portray a sense of anxiety and foreboding. Use dynamic variation to try to emphasize this.

- The accents on the chords in bars 5, 6 and 7 indicate that these should be played strongly to create a striking contrast against the quieter bass notes in those bars.

- The key signature is E minor, although notes outside the key – F natural and B flat – are used to extend the harmonic range.

Spring

[Group A]

Antonio Vivaldi
(1678 – 1741)

Minuet

[Group A]

Johann Sebastian Bach
(1685 – 1750)

7

Là Ci Darem La Mano

Wolfgang Amadeus Mozart
(1756 - 1791)

[Group A]

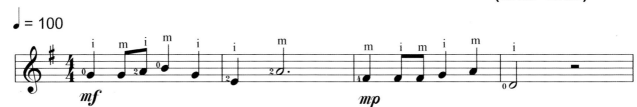

© Copyright 2002 by Registry Publications

William Tell Overture

Gioacchino Rossini
(1792 - 1868)

[Group A]

© Copyright 1997 by Registry Publications

8

Malagueña

[Group B]

Traditional Spanish

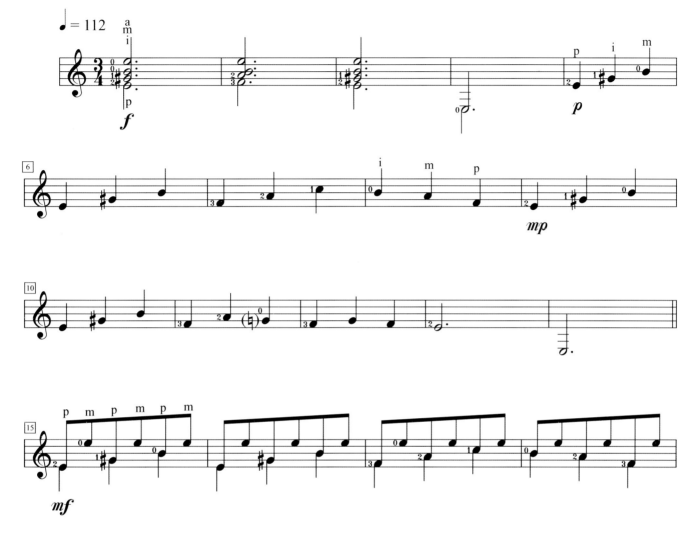

The Chase

[Group B]

Raymond Burley
(1948 –)

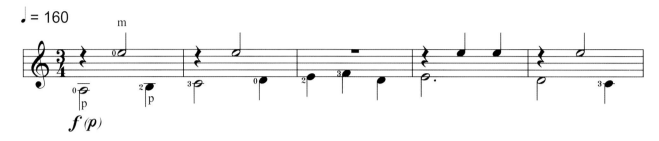

10

In A Rush

[Group B]

Franz Biederman
(1958 –)

Tension In The Air

[Group B]

Tony Skinner
(1960 –)

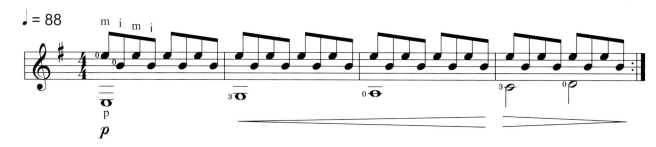

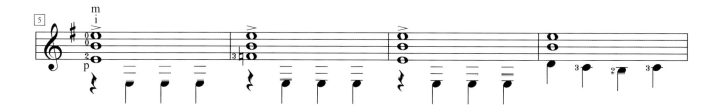

VIVA VOCE

The examiner will ask questions, based on the music performed, to test the candidate's knowledge of the stave, bar lines, notes and rests, key and time signatures, accidentals and dynamics. The information below provides a summary of the information that is required. A maximum of 15 marks may be awarded in this section of the examination.

The stave

The notes on the lines (E G B D F) can be remembered by making up an unusual phrase such as: **E**normous **G**uitarists **B**reak **D**ainty **F**ootstools
The notes in the spaces between the lines form the word **FACE**.

Bar lines

A bar is a way of dividing music into manageable portions. It makes music easier to read and makes it easier to discover where the main beat lies. The end of each bar is indicated by a vertical line called a *bar line*. The space between each pair of bar lines, where the notes are written, is called a bar (also known as a *measure*). At the end of the last bar, or a section, of a piece of music there are two vertical lines. These are called a *double bar line*.

Notes and rests

The table below shows the names of the notes and rests, and their values. (You can use either the traditional or modern terminology when identifying notes).

Traditional name	Modern name	Note	Rest	Value in crotchet beats
semibreve	whole note	𝅝	▬	4
dotted minim	dotted half note	𝅗𝅥·	▬·	3
minim	half note	𝅗𝅥	▬	2
crotchet	quarter note	𝅘𝅥	𝄽	1
quaver	eighth note	𝅘𝅥𝅮	𝄾	½

Time signatures

The numbers that appear at the beginning of a piece of music are called the time signature. The top number shows the number of beats per bar, whilst the bottom number indicates the value of each beat. For example, $\frac{4}{4}$ means four crotchet beats (i.e. four quarter notes) per bar, whilst $\frac{3}{4}$ means three crotchet beats per bar.

 3 crotchet beats per bar

 4 crotchet beats per bar

Key signatures

C major or A minor

Where there is one sharp at the beginning of each stave of a piece of music, this indicates that the key is either G major or E minor. Where there is no visible key signature the key will be C major or A minor.

G major or E minor

You can sometimes establish whether the key is major or minor by looking at the first and final notes of the piece. For example, in a piece with a key signature of one sharp, if the first and last note is G (as in *Spring*) then it is likely that the piece is in the key of G major, rather than E minor.

- When one sharp occurs in a key signature it will always be on the top F line, and indicates that all F notes throughout the piece should be played as F#.

A sharp or flat that occurs during a piece of music, rather than as part of the key signature, is called an **accidental**. It has the effect of sharpening or flattening that note and any others at the same pitch within the same bar. It does not affect notes in the following bar. In the final bars of *Tension In The Air* a B flat accidental note occurs. In the same piece a **natural** sign occurs in bar 6. The function of a natural sign is to cancel any preceding sharps or flats applied to that note. In this instance, the natural sign is used to cancel the F sharp that appears in the key signature and consequently the F note in bar 6 should be played as F natural.

Dynamic markings

Dynamic markings indicate how softly or strongly to play:

> *p* is short for piano – meaning 'soft' (quiet).

> *f* is short for forte – meaning 'strong' (loud).

> *m* is short for 'mezzo' (i.e. half) – meaning 'moderately'. *m* does not occur on its own, but can be combined with *f* or *p*: *mf* means 'moderately strong', *mp* means 'moderately soft'.

> This sign ◁──────── means *crescendo* (get louder).

> This sign ────────▷ means *diminuendo* (get quieter).

> This sign **>** above a note or chord is an accent sign, which means the note(s) should be stressed.

UNIVERSITY OF
WEST LONDON

LONDON COLLEGE OF MUSIC EXAMINATIONS

Classical Guitar
Examination Entry Form

STEP 2

The standard LCM Exams music entry form is NOT valid for Classical Guitar entries.
Entry to the examination is only possible via this original form.
Photocopies of this form will not be accepted under any circumstances.

For candidates making online entries for classical guitar examinations, the handbook entry form must still be completed and must be submitted by post before the entry deadline to:
For UK and Ireland entries: LCM Exams, University of West London, St Mary's Road, Ealing, London, W5 5RF, UK.
For entries not from the UK and Ireland: the completed entry form should be sent to your local LCM Exams Representative.

Please use black ink and block capital letters when completing this form.

SESSION (Spring/Summer/Winter): _____ YEAR:_____

Preferred Examination Centre (if known): _____
If left blank you will be examined at the nearest venue to your home address.

Candidate Details:

Candidate Name (as to appear on certificate):

_____

Candidate ID (if entered previously): _____ Date of birth: _____

Gender (M/F): _____Ethnicity (see chart overleaf):_____
Date of birth and ethnicity details are for statistical purposes only, and are not passed on to the examiner.

☐ Tick this box if you are attaching details of particular needs requirements.

Teacher Details:

Teacher Name (as to appear on certificate): _____

Teacher Qualifications (if required on certificate): _____

LCM Teacher Code (if entered previously): _____

Address: _____

_____ Postcode: _____

Tel. No. (day): _____(evening): _____

Email Address: _____

☐ Tick this box if any details above have changed since your last LCM entry.

IMPORTANT NOTES

- It is the candidate's responsibility to have knowledge of, and comply with, the current syllabus requirements. Where candidates are entered for examinations by a teacher, the teacher must take responsibility that candidates are entered in accordance with the current syllabus requirements. Failure to carry out any of the examination requirements may lead to disqualification.

- For candidates with particular needs, a letter giving details and requests for any special requirements (e.g. enlarged sight reading), together with an official supporting document (e.g. medical certificate), should be attached.

- Examinations may be held on any day of the week, including weekends. Any appointment requests (e.g. 'prefer morning,' or 'prefer weekdays') must be made at the time of entry. **LCM Exams and its Representatives will take note of the information given; however, no guarantees can be made that all wishes can be met.**

- Submission of this entry is an undertaking to abide by the current regulations.

Examination Fee: £ _____

Late Entry Fee (if necessary)   £ _____

Total amount submitted: £ _____

If already entered and paid on-line, tick here: _____

Cheques or postal orders should be made payable to '*University of West London*'.
A list of current fees, entry deadlines and session dates is available from LCM Exams.

Where to submit your entry form

**Entries for public centres should be sent to the
LCM Exams local examination centre representative
(NOT to the LCM Exams Head Office).**

View the LCM Exams website www.uwl.ac.uk/lcmexams
or contact the LCM Exams office (tel: 020 8231 2364 / email: lcm.exams@uwl.ac.uk)
for details of your nearest local examination centre representative.

**Entries for private centres, should be sent direct to:
LCM Exams, University of West London, St Mary's Road, Ealing, London, W5 5RF**

Official Entry Form